GILLIAN SLOVO

South African-born Gillian Slovo has lived in England since 1964. She is a novelist, journalist and memoirist. Her work in theatre includes *Another World: Losing our Children to Islamic State* at the National Theatre; and *The Riots* at the Tricycle. Her novels include five crime novels featuring her detective Kate Baeier and, as well, *Ties of Blood*, *The Betrayal*, *Red Dust* (which won France's Temoin du Monde), *Ice Road* (shortlisted for the 2004 Orange Prize for Fiction), *Black Orchids* and *Ten Days*. Her family memoir *Every Secret Thing: My Family, My Country* was a world bestseller. She has been the President of English PEN and is a fellow of the Royal Society of Literature.

Gillian Slovo

GRENFELL
in the words of survivors

NICK HERN BOOKS
London
www.nickhernbooks.co.uk

A Nick Hern Book

Grenfell: in the words of survivors first published in Great Britain as a paperback original in 2023 by Nick Hern Books Limited, The Glasshouse, 49a Goldhawk Road, London W12 8QP

Grenfell: in the words of survivors copyright © 2023 Gillian Slovo
Documentary transcript (pp. 90–95) copyright © 2023 Royal National Theatre

Cover image: Illustration by Anthony Burrill; Art direction and design by National Theatre Graphic Design Studio

Designed and typeset by Nick Hern Books, London
Printed in Great Britain by Mimeo Ltd, Huntingdon, Cambridgeshire PE29 6XX

A CIP catalogue record for this book is available from the British Library

ISBN 978 1 83904 263 8

www.nickhernbooks.co.uk/environmental-policy

Introduction
Gillian Slovo

In the early hours of 14 June 2017 a resident of flat 16 on the fourth floor of Grenfell Tower telephoned 999 to tell them that his fridge had caught fire. The resident then did everything right: he got all the occupants of his flat, and his floor, out of the building. Four fire engines were also quickly on the scene. Everybody assumed that the fire would soon be out. There had, after all, been previous fires in Grenfell and all of them had been extinguished without loss of life. But this time was different. The fire, which had leaked through the window of flat 16, began to climb up the building. So rapidly did it move that within twenty minutes, one whole side of the twenty-four-floor tower was alight.

The fire didn't stop there. It crossed the roof and spread down the opposite side. As people who were outside watched in horror, calling at friends and relatives to get out, Grenfell Tower was soon completely consumed by fire. 'Stay put' was the UK's standard advice to people in high-rises – that they stay in the flat unless the fire starts in their flat or close by it – and it proved disastrous. This orthodoxy, combined with the rapid spread of fire and the Fire Brigade's initial failure to recognise what was happening and evacuate the building, resulted in the loss of the lives of seventy-one of the building's residents – which rose to seventy-two when the final victim died.

Almost as soon as the fire was out, we knew that the cladding that had been used to line the building in a recent refurbishment, and that also made up the decorative crown on the roof, was the reason that the fire had spread so fast. We knew this because there had been other cladding fires in Britain and worldwide. None of them had, however, resulted in such a loss of life. Three months after the fire, the government set up a public inquiry whose job it was to find out how this could have happened in one of the richest boroughs, in one of the richest cities, in the world. The Inquiry sat for four hundred days, published a first report and is, at the time of writing, preparing its second report.

The Inquiry has uncovered an astonishing catalogue of failures. The refurbishment of Grenfell Tower that was completed in 2016, a year before the fire, had turned a previously non-flammable concrete building into a graveyard. A succession of witnesses – architects, fire inspectors, employees of the Tenant Management Organisation that managed the building, council employees, builders, the companies that made the cladding and insulation, and many more – were all exposed as having failed in a way that contributed to that fire. So many of them, in fact, that what the main QC to the Inquiry called 'a merry-go-round of buck-passing' which made it difficult to point the finger in any one direction.

The Inquiry did a sterling job of exposing these multiple failures. We can only hope that the government takes their recommendations seriously – as they have not so far done. But behind the facts of who failed, what went wrong and why it did, are the people of Grenfell, their relatives and friends, and the whole community around them, who suffered such devastating losses. Their voices were absent in the days after the fire. They were too busy trying to do for each other what both local and central government failed to do, and they were too affected by what had happened. Instead we got sound bites and mischaracterisations of who this community was by a media searching only for sensation and all too often by the temptation to victim-blame. This absence of their voices was made worse by the fact that many people who lived in the tower had known something was going wrong, had tried to tell the council this, and had been not only ignored but also insulted.

This is why I, and the National Theatre, set out to produce this play. Because we wanted to let the words of the survivors and bereaved ring out on a public stage. This is a verbatim play, which means that it is based on the words from interviews I have made, along with extracts from the Inquiry or from the public record. Over the time that I have worked on this play I interviewed many people – survivors, bereaved, witnesses, experts and others – to collect the raw materials for the text.

I couldn't use everybody I interviewed, but everybody I spoke to helped me understand what had happened at Grenfell Tower. The words I did use, with the interviewees' permission, are heavily edited but always with the aim of keeping the actual words and their meaning.

It has been an enormous privilege for me to get to know some of these people, and to understand their wider community. Given what they have suffered, their generosity to us, and to the world, is astonishing. The play that I have fashioned is only a small part of what they, and others who are not in the play, have to tell and teach us. I hope it helps amplify their call for justice, not only that those who are responsible for what happened are held accountable for their crimes, but also for a change in the way we all live and the things we too readily accept. I hope that those who read this play will also experience some of the privilege I have experienced at meeting these wonderful people. I also hope that they will be encouraged by the inspiring story of a community who, in the most devastating of circumstances, came together to help each other, and who continue to campaign so that no one should suffer as they have suffered.

London,
June 2023

Grenfell: in the words of survivors was first performed in the Dorfman auditorium of the National Theatre, London, on 20 July 2023 (previews from 13 July). The cast in alphabetical order was as follows:

ANTONIO RONCOLATO	Joe Alessi
MAHER KHOUDAIR	Gaz Choudhry
JUDITH BLAKEMAN	Jackie Clune
RABIA YAHYA	Houda Echouafni
TIAGO ALVES	Keaton Guimarães-Tolley
NICK BURTON	Ash Hunter
NATASHA ELCOCK	Pearl Mackie
BELLAL EL-GUENUNI	Rachid Sabitri
HANAN WAHABI	Sarah Slimani
EDWARD DAFFARN	Michael Shaeffer
TURUFAT YILMA	Nahel Tzegai
HANAN / RABIA (*Alternate*)	Lisa Zahra

With very special thanks to Mona Goodwin.

Contributors: Feruza Afewerki, Tiago Alves, Judith Blakeman, Nick Burton, Edward Daffarn, Natasha Elcock, Bellal El-Guenuni, Fatima El-Guenuni, Maher Khoudair, Karim Mussilhy, Antonio Roncolato, Rabia Yahya, Turufat Yilma and Hanan Wahabi

Lakanal House clip voice-over	Gunnar Cauthery
999 call voice-over	Michael Workeye

Directors	Phyllida Lloyd
	and Anthony Simpson-Pike
Set and Costume Designer	Georgia Lowe
Lighting Designer	Azusa Ono
Sound Designer	Donato Wharton
Video Designer	Akhila Krishnan
Composer	Benjamin Kwasi Burrell
Additional Music	Brain Rays

Movement Director	Chi-San Howard
Casting	Chandra Ruegg
	and Alastair Coomer CDG
Voice and Dialect Coach	Hazel Holder
Staff Director	Aaliyah Mckay
Head of Welfare and Wellbeing	Jess Dickens
Wellbeing Practitioner	Ashley Miller
Dramatherapist	Patricia Ojehonmon

Developed with the National Theatre's New Work Department.

Film created in collaboration with TEA films.

MUSICIANS

Violin	Ruth Elder
Viola	Nicola Hicks
Baritone Saxophone	Jessamy Holder
Cello	Zara Hudon-Kozdoj
Double Bass	Charlie Pyne
Bass Clarinet	Nick Moss
Tenor Saxophone	Guy Passey

Recorded at Air Edel Recording Studio and engineered by Nick Taylor with Olly Thompson.

Guitars	Ed Riches

Recorded at the National Theatre.

Author's Note

For any Inquiry moments I have included the date of that dialogue for checking and accuracy purposes. There is no reason that the audience needs continually to be told of these dates.

Public-sector information licensed under the Open Government Licence v3.0 nationalarchives.gov.uk/doc/open-government-licence/version/3/ including:

- Evidence from the Grenfell Tower Inquiry
- Extracts from transcripts of calls made to the control room officers on 14 June 2017 by Belhailu Kebede, Rabia Yahya, Natasha Elcock, Denis Murphy, Katarzyna Dabrowska and others

This play also contains extracts from the witness statements of Michael Dowden, Jamal Stern, Hanan Wahabi, Assistant Operations Manager Alexandra Norman and Nick Burton and radio comms from LFB00024348_Operational Response Report Version 0.3a.pdf, London Fire Brigade (Grenfell Tower Inquiry).

This play contains information of Opus 2 International Limited licensed under the Opus 2 Grenfell Tower Inquiry Licence, and public-sector information licensed under the Open Government Licence.

Thanks

Edward Daffarn for permission to quote from the Grenfell Action Blog.

Peter Apps for his considerable help with this play and for allowing us to use his words from our interview without direct attribution to him.

Lee Hall for his involvement in the planning stages, and his participation in many of the interviews that help make up the words of this play.

And the many people from the tower and the wider community, and also outside experts who I interviewed. Despite that I couldn't get everybody in the play, all of them helped me understand what had happened on that night, and why it happened.

Characters

Former residents of Grenfell Tower

NATASHA ELCOCK
RABIA YAHYA
HANAN WAHABI
TURUFAT YILMA
TIAGO ALVES
ANTONIO RONCOLATO
EDWARD (ED) DAFFARN
MAHER KHOUDAIR
NICHOLAS (NICK) BURTON

Political figures

DAVID CAMERON (*on screen*)
MARGARET THATCHER (*on screen*)
JUDITH BLAKEMAN
FRANCES KIRKHAM (*through a letter*)
ERIC PICKLES (*through a letter*)

Inquiry evidence

QC (*Inquiry lawyer – generic*)
BRIAN MARTIN
DAVID GIBSON
STEPHEN BLAKE
SIMON LAWRENCE
CREW MANAGER JAMAL STERN
WATCH MANAGER MICHAEL DOWDEN
ASSISTANT OPERATIONS MANAGER ALEXANDRA
    NORMAN
CONTROL ROOM OPERATOR HEIDI FOX
CONTROL ROOM OPERATOR PETER DUDDY
CONTROL ROOM OPERATOR ANGELA GOTTS

CLAUDE SCHMIDT
RAY BAILEY
JONATHON ROPER
PAUL EVANS
IVOR MEREDITH
PHILIP HEATH
DIANE MARSHALL
FIREFIGHTER GREGORY LAWSON
ASSISTANT COMMISSIONER ANDY ROE

This text went to press before the end of rehearsals and so may differ slightly from the play as performed.

ACT ONE

The cast come one by one through the audience and onto the stage.

CAST MEMBER (NATASHA ELCOCK). My name is [*cast member name*].

I play Natasha Elcock who lived with her family in flat eighty-two, on the eleventh floor of Grenfell Tower.

My words are taken from interviews with Natasha, and with her consent.

CAST MEMBER (ANTONIO RONCOLATO). Most of our words come from interviews, but sometimes they're from the public Inquiry, and occasionally we'll speak as ourselves. I'm [*cast member name*].

I play Antonio Roncolato, who lived with his son in flat seventy-two on the tenth floor – so the flat directly below Natasha's.

CAST MEMBER (HANAN WAHABI). My name is [*cast member name*] and I'm playing Hanan Wahabi, who lived with her family in flat sixty-six on the ninth floor.

Hanan's brother Abdulaziz el-Wahabi and his family also lived in Grenfell Tower – in flat one-eight-two – in a line with Natasha's and Antonio's but higher up, on the twenty-first floor.

CAST MEMBER (RABIA YAHYA). My name is [*cast member name*].

I play Rabia Yahya, who lived on the eighteenth floor in flat one-five-two – so on the same side of the building as Antonio and Natasha and Abdulaziz. She lived there with her husband Bellal and their three children.

CAST MEMBER (BELLAL EL-GUENUNI). I'm playing Rabia's husband, Bellal El-Guenuni. My name is [*cast member name*].

CAST MEMBER (TURUFAT YILMA). I'm *[cast member name]*. I play Turufat Yilma, who lived with her family in flat forty-four, on the seventh floor.

CAST MEMBER (TIAGO ALVES). I'm *[cast member name]*. I play Tiago Alves, who lived with his family in flat one-oh-five on the thirteenth floor.

CAST MEMBER (NICK BURTON). I play Nick Burton, who lived with his wife Pily and their dog, Lewis Hamilton the Second, in flat one-six-five on the nineteenth floor. So Nick would be on the same side of the building as Tiago's family but six floors up.

My name is *[cast member name]*.

CAST MEMBER (ED DAFFARN). And I'm *[cast member name]*. I play Edward Daffarn, who lived in flat one-three-four on the sixteenth floor.

CAST MEMBER (MAHER KHOUDAIR). My name is *[cast member name]*. I play Maher Khoudair, who lived in flat sixty-four on the ninth floor – so in a one-bedroom flat in a line with Ed's but seven floors down. When he was interviewed, Maher spoke in Arabic but I will be speaking in English. Also, Maher uses crutches to walk because of his disability.

CAST MEMBER (JUDITH BLAKEMAN). I play Judith Blakeman, a Labour councillor.

My name is *[cast member name]*.

CAST MEMBER. This is as much a story of a community as of a fire. We are a community as well and we invite you to turn to the person next to you and introduce yourself.

CAST MEMBER. Thank you and welcome, everyone. Can I just take this opportunity to reassure you that we won't be showing any images of fire.

CAST MEMBER. If you want to leave, even for a short break, our front-of-house staff will show you out. There'll be someone to talk with you if that's what you'd like.

CAST MEMBER. If you do leave, you're welcome to come back. Someone will tell you when that's possible and they'll help you back to your seat.

On screen the words:

'4th April 2011.

Six years, two months and ten days before the fire.'

DAVID CAMERON. One of the key aims of this coalition is to massively reduce the number of rules, laws and regulations that frankly treat all of you like idiots. They don't just drive you mad, they're often obstacles to everything we need as a country. We need businesses to grow and take people on, but these regulations cost businesses time and money. There are over twenty-one-thousand statutory rules and regulations currently in force in our country and I want us to bring the overall burden of regulation down. And fast. From now on, the presumption will be that regulations will go unless someone has a good reason for them to stay. But even this on its own is not enough. We need to apply real pressure on ministers to scrap these regulations and this is where you come in.[1]

A group of citizens fumbling to recover what has been lost.

A reconstruction.

NATASHA ELCOCK *(flat 82, eleventh floor)*. I could see my white wind… my white flowers in the window. And I remember saying my flowers are still out. And for days I kept saying, my flowers are still on the window. They were just a pound-shop bunch.

TURUFAT YILMA *(flat 44, seventh floor)*. I had quite a few things that remind me back home – ornament, could be a poster or even postcard. We have that piece of material we put so your seat doesn't get dirty, so again with that piece of textile you made a design out of that. So it's like a bit of tradition thing, bright colours, a mixture of yellow, green and blue which is stand out. Especially green is. It's, it's, it's a hope.

HANAN WAHABI (*flat 66, ninth floor*). My son Zak painted his bedroom a very dark Moroccan red. When he wanted to change it, it took a lot of coats. I had some, some nice paintings up, one of them one of them was like a nice red boat with like the sunsets and I had some Arabic calligraphy as well, because I am very spiritual.

TIAGO ALVES (*flat 105, thirteenth floor*). My mum, having worked as a professional housekeeper, everything has to be pretty much spotless and clean. I didn't keep a clean room, to the disappointment of my mum.

If I close my eyes and try to remember our flat I don't really know why now the one thing that really does come to my mind is I had this really big whiteboard and er it was always filled with equations of sorts because what I tended to do, I think I tended to write and take a couple of steps back and just like observe. It was never static. I liked the nonpermanence of it. It gave me a bit of freedom I guess.

And the bookshelf we had at the front door. It was full of my mum's religious texts and mixed in with them were my scientific texts. Some of my comic books as well. *Captain America*: I was a big Captain America fan.

HANAN. Even though I was on the sixth floor you do have that skyline, because you're, you're just above the trees. Obviously. I wear my hijab, my headscarf. I didn't have to wear it because no one can really see you anyway.

NATASHA. Great positioning for New Year's Eve, the fireworks. Um, you'd watch it as it happened and on the TV at the same time so you could get a bit of a delay.

TIAGO. And basically, you could, I was just trying to think of. Urm, I don't know how to explain it, but it just looked like London.

HANAN. I spent my whole life in the Royal Borough of Kensington and Chelsea. I moved into Grenfell in October 2001. I was very pleased with the space and the fact that, my brother and his family were upstairs. Yeah. And not too far from where my mum was.

I've got three sisters who live on the Lancaster West Estate, which is the estate that Grenfell was on. And we used to, you could wave from each other's flats. And my parents were in walking distance.

ED DAFFARN (*flat 134, sixteenth floor*). When I got my flat in Grenfell Tower my heart told me it was going to be okay. I was really, really happy and yeah, no, it was good, it was good, it was a you know it was good. They really were beautiful. And so spacious.

I was also aware that you know tower blocks are made of concrete. Most people are just like see a tower block and say I can't move there it's blah blah, but in fact what people don't understand is as soon as you close your front door it's so peaceful.

TURUFAT. I'm from Ethiopia. The political unrest that was the reason I left my hometown. I came to England, I was under the age, I was fifteen. When I was nineteen, I got a one-bedroom in Grenfell. I was really, really happy. It's just, it was my safest place.

MAHER. I'm from Syria. I came to England in 2001. I loved it, and I still do. I consider it my second homeland, seeing as I've got the nationality now.

I had polio when I was five years old and I have problems in my legs now. [I was in unsuitable housing so the council] gave me the option to start 'bidding'. There were various flats that they showed me, but there were other people before me on the list and, every time, they'd get the flat.

Then I got a text message about Grenfell Tower which said: 'You're first on the list, go and see it.' I called them and said, 'What's the place like?' They said it was ground floor, maybe first floor.

When I went to see it they told me it was in fact on the sixth floor. They said, 'We've got two lifts in the building. You won't have any trouble, these two lifts are always working.' So I said 'Okay, I'll take it.'

When the war happened in Syria, I was scared for my kids and my wife, because the fighting came very close to them so I decided to bring them to join me in the UK.

RABIA YAHYA (*flat 152, eighteenth floor*). I was born into Grenfell Tower. We lived there until I was twelve and then because we needed more room we moved.

NATASHA. I was born on the estate. I actually lived there all my life.

NICK BURTON (*flat 165, nineteenth floor*). I was born just a couple of blocks away. I could see the tower from where I lived.

NATASHA. We used to play Knock Down Ginger up and down the tower.

NICK. Everybody in everybody's house, everybody had their key on a piece of string through the letterbox.

RABIA. When I was a kid there, we did play out on the landings because it was safe you know.

We'd all bring out our own toys, dolls, and skates – roller skates. We just sort of did laps, going around and taking it in turns cos it was just one skates and everyone would want a turn. Regardless of that, even though they were mine, they would just, we would all share it, all our stuff with the other neighbours.

After Bellal and I got married, we had Naila, and when she was two we were offered flat one-five-two. I was over the moon to be living back in Grenfell.

BELLAL EL-GUENUNI (*flat 152, eighteenth floor*). Our second and third were born there.

So normally when you go into a new block or a new estate you kind of think that I don't know maybe you could have issues, you could have, your, your normal problems that you might in tower blocks or estates.

NATASHA. Obviously, people's preconceptions of an estate is, it's, you know, gangs of kids running up and down and it wasn't like that at all. It really wasn't.

BELLAL. Grenfell was slightly different. Neighbours were respect, respectful, they were professionals, there were a lot of people working, lot of families, a lot of kids. It had its challenges but on the whole it was a nice place to live.

NATASHA. It was a tower block, but it was home.

RABIA. It was perfect ideal for me like cos I knew a lot of people who lived in the tower and obviously you know day in day out, when you see people daily, you know, waiting for the lift, you still do make friends very quickly.

HANAN. Me and my next-door neighbour Natalie kept the doors open so children can go in and out. We would sit on the landing actually have cups of tea – English Breakfast, English Breakfast girls – I was raised on PG Tips – and see the children playing.

And then obviously, I felt, you know, it was okay for the children to go upstairs. They regularly were up on my brother's floor.

TURUFAT. It's not that we knock each other door to have coffee or tea but the fact that you feel that safe and surrounded by those kind of neighbours.

NICK. It was a community. A true layer-upon-layer of communities integrating and becoming just one community.

RABIA. Every floor had smells of different cuisines. And different music. Moroccan music on the top floor and then the middle layer someone listening to reggae music.

MAHER. The tower was one big family. Anything we asked for, people would bring it. Even things – in Ramadan, people brought us things, I wasn't expecting that. People knew [my family] were coming from a war zone, so they would help us a lot.

I was a keen table tennis player in Syria and I used to win first places in tournaments. When I was in Grenfell I had a table tennis coach and used to play with people with disabilities.

NICK. We used to go as a group, we'd just go to Pily's flat on the old sixteenth floor of the tower block.

It wasn't actually about Pily right at the beginning because I thought oh my god, she won't like a little a little boy like me but I could go and play cards with her parents. Like, like a little bit of gambling.

Pily was a little bit older than me and um and way out of my league. It was just like, an older woman.

She was very beautiful; my wife was beautiful. You know she could have chosen anybody really; she was very flamboyant. Talked to everybody and I mean everybody, she doesn't hold back. She was the first person if you get into a lift she'll say hello, how are you to everybody. But she just you know liked me, I don't know why.

Within a month or so I'd moved in. You know sock by sock. My mum had said where's all your clothes? So, I went I've got a, I've got a girlfriend and it's like and she's like your age.

TIAGO. I was quite well-known in the tower for being someone who did quite well in my studies. I'm not trying to blow my own trumpet or anything but one encounter someone said, 'I heard you did really well in the tests' and the person was like 'You can actually make a name for us.' What he meant by 'us' was the local community.

It felt like my success was not only my success it was not only my family's success but the success of the local neighbourhood because everyone was so interconnected and so you kind of band together in the struggles but you also revel in the successes of everyone else around you and like because you would spend a lot of time waiting for lifts and stuff you would get to know your community more than you probably would anywhere else in London.

One particular memory, it was around September time and there was a boy who was really struggling to get his tie on, he was obviously his first day in secondary school and his mum turned to me and said 'Do you mind teaching him how to do a tie?' and so I took off my tie and I told him to follow my instructions step by step and eventually got the tie on and I told him 'When you get home try it a couple of times.' Unfortunately he ended up passing away in the fire.

NICK. My father came from St Lucia to drive the buses.

NATASHA. My dad was also an immigrant. His mum came over on *Windrush*. My mum's white, my mum's English, probably what you would deem was kind of poor. My great grandmother had a stall on Portobello, a fruit and veg stall. And my great-grandad worked. My nan worked. And they lived there all their life.

NICK. After people from the Caribbean other communities came in: the Moroccans, the Spanish, the Portuguese.

TIAGO. There was quite a decent Portuguese community in the local area. I only started learning English when I went to school and part of the reason because my parents were scared that I was gonna gain their accent from them.

ANTONIO RONCOLATO (*flat 72, tenth floor*). I was born in Padua. It's in the north-east of Italy not too far from Venice. I came to London in 25th of January 1984 and I've been there, I've been here ever since. So, basically, I liked it too much.

I was employed at the Millennium Gloucester Hotel. So, I've been spending all my working life here, I'm a restaurant manager.

I moved into Grenfell Tower in, ah, that was it, in October 1990 with my wife at that time, who was from Colombia. We spent the first night in there when my son came out of the hospital, basically. Christopher, my son, spent his whole life in, in, in, in Grenfell Tower.

Christopher will be twenty-eight this year in October.

I'm a Londoner. I'm, I'm Italian but I spent I mean, thirty-odd years in London. So, basically this is my city, this is my town, this is my place. It will be a hypocrite of me to say I'm English. No, I'm not. I'm Italian but I like London, I like England, I love England. From London I am on top of the world. If you allow me a little bit of arrogance, ah, it's like I can see any other city from like this, from above. Okay? Little Padua there, little Masera, little Berlin, so-and-so, gay Paris here but I'm in London, so I'm on top. You know, this is London to me. This is my area, Kensington and Chelsea.

NICK. It's a very different place from my youth even if it is still a melting pot.

It's really kind of weird like when I started reading the newspapers like oh the poor or second-class citizens or illegal immigrants in the tower I was like really that's not what happened there it's just normal people. But there are roads in Kensington and Chelsea that's not Millionaires' Road, it's Billionaires' Road. Like if you've, you know just ripped off your country or you'd done some dirty dealings around the world and you want to kind of wash your money, you buy a property and then you just leave it because now it's fresh money now, it's bricks and mortar.

But the youth and the people you know that live like in North Kensington, most of them just work on minimum wage trying to get by.

NATASHA. If you look at the view from the tower, two streets up, Robbie Williams owns a house. I don't necessarily live next door to David Beckham, but I live five minutes away from him. You know, David Cameron is literally three streets up and has lived there for many years. Boris Johnson's sister lives across the way.

I never classified it as a rich or poor area, I never see it, saw it as a deprived area, I just saw it as a council estate in the middle of Notting Hill. It's only since June 14th, that you start to think, oh my god we were categorised as poor.

I was always really proud. I'd say, I live in the Royal Borough of Kensington and Chelsea. Not many people out there can say they live in the Royal Borough. Since the fire obviously, my viewpoints on the fact that it's the Royal Borough has changed.

TIAGO. In 2001 my parents were both in steady jobs, and they, you know my dad's ambition had always been to purchase property here in London. So he bought our flat using the Right to Buy scheme. And he's always said to me that it was probably the best thing he has ever done in his life. In terms of mentally speaking, he felt like he was the, the author of his own destiny.

JUDITH BLAKEMAN. Kensington and Chelsea has always been a Conservative borough. But North Kensington, the poorest part of the borough, did have Labour councillors. I'm one of them and I had special responsibility for dealing with Grenfell Tower and so I sat on Kensington and Chelsea's Tenant Management Organisation's board.

Most Tenant Management Organisations tend to cover one or two blocks or a small estate. This covered the whole of the borough, it became a huge bureaucracy. And it became more and more unresponsive to the actual tenants as the time went by.

BELLAL. You started to notice that there was quite yeah, a few issues with the lift and breaking down and stopping which made our life er quite hard.

ED. If we complained about anything the Tenants Management Organisation and the council kind of came after us.

BELLAL. I think the, the feeling that you get is kind of um you should be grateful for getting a flat in the first place and kind of beggars can't be choosers. So it was little bit like yeah you don't really wanna push it.

Our whole sink was kind of lopsided to a certain degree where I don't know if the wood had started to erode. But when we called them in, what they came and done was er they refused to change the whole unit.

MAN. That one's broke, that one's fine…

BELLAL. So that would stay. They just changed the one door on, on so yeah had different kind of coloured doors along the kitchen.

It was more or less you were talking to another human being that has got all the power. So if you were to call one of them and you were to speak to them in a way that they didn't like or you were a little bit upset or something then you stand no chance even if it's your, your right even if it's, it's, it's urgent. They would lock you off like they are above the law like they don't have no obligation towards you. So, you have to be very careful how you speak to them.

MAHER. I had a one-bedroom flat for the whole family: me, my wife, and our three daughters. With five people, that's impossible. We asked for a different flat, but nothing happened.

I had to buy a bunk bed for the living room and put up a screen around them. My kids slept there, behind the screen, actually a curtain.

JUDITH. We had a meeting on the 17th of November 2008 erm when two officers from the council told us that they were looking at the housing revenue account. They wanted a new sport centre, a new secondary school, a restoration of the old street pattern: that was really controversial. Erm they said that they were appointing master planners to look at the options.

Flash up the plan graphics:

'Notting Barns Master Plan 2009.'

A map of the area should accompany this, outlining the study area.

'Notting Barns Master Plan 2009: the study area sits adjacent to some of the most prime residential land in the country. Socially the area could be transformed and this would capitalise on its location. We estimate that the project could deliver significant returns to the council.

Grenfell Tower: we consider that the appearance of this building and the way in which it meets the ground blights much of the area east of Latimer Road Station. On balance our preferred approach is to assume demolition.'

I think basically they thought it was quite disgraceful that all this land was wasted on social housing. They started to run down the estates because they wanted to redevelop them and change the whole social fabric of North Kensington.

NICK. From the late eighties the area started to change. And after 1999 after the film *Notting Hill* the whole thing just went boom.

It was a trendy place to be and so they'd buy the properties up and people would cash in and move out.

ED. A lot of the kind of estates that now exist in North Kensington the land was compulsorily purchased from kind of the likes of slum landlords and turned into council properties.

People were relieved when the council built proper housing on them. It was kind of much more recently that a much more unhealthy policy started. So once a local authority was there to act as some sort of guardian, some sort of custodian. But that wasn't what we got into, we got into this highly exploited kind of mantra, sweating the assets in North Kensington.

I believe there was an ideology: why should these people live in this area of London? I mean personally I think it was about a kind of warped uh neo-con political philosophy. They didn't have to dig for the gold they simply had to marginalise the people living on the land and that's what they were doing.

JUDITH. They never put the Notting Barns Plan into effect. They told us it was just an aspiration, I mean, they never gave us any reason.

ED. We had three smallish AstroTurf football pitches to the north of the tower, and a large car park to the right of that. It was all neglected and run down but it was ours.

JUDITH: They then said, 'We're going to build a new academy on the football pitches and the car park in the Lancaster West Estate.' A lot of the residents were upset about that.

HANAN. Before the school was built I could see the children playing football from my window. I also used to play football on those same pitches. The academy took out all our space, all our greenery and our pitches.

JUDITH. We came forward with all sorts of alternatives and the answer always was 'no we have to build a new school, it has to be new to meet the conditions of the "building schools for the future" [scheme]'.

NATASHA. For me the only reason why I can see that the tower was redone was to fit in visually with the [new] school and sports centre. For no other reason than that.

MAHER. It certainly looked nicer than before but that was it. As if you'd taken this cup and covered it in gold. The cover is better, but that's all.

CAST MEMBER. When Grenfell was built, its walls were concrete. For the refurb, they wanted to make the building more sustainable and energy efficient and they also wanted it to look better so they decided to put up a cladding system.

It consisted of a cladding panel, insulation and a gap between the two so the rain water could drain through.

The insulation, which was flammable, was fixed to the concrete wall. The gap acted as a chimney on the night of the fire. Because of the cladding and insulation, the new walls were further out and the new windows had also to be moved out. The new windows were made of unplasticised polyvinyl chloride, or UPVC, which was also very flammable. They also put flammable insulation in the gap between the window sill and the new windows, and pretty much stuck a piece of plastic over the window sill as well.

ED. The Grenfell Action Group was formed um, kind of in response to the academy project and also fears about other regeneration. We started a blog in 2012, I think it was June 2012.

Grenfell Action Group Blog.

14th August 2012.[3]

Four years, ten months before the fire.

'Dear Royal Borough of Kensington and Chelsea Councillors,

The Grenfell Action Group would like to extend a warm invitation to all the Borough Councillors to visit Lancaster West Estate for an informal walkabout to see with your own eyes how our housing estate has been allowed to deteriorate into a near slum.'

The whole thing had kind of fallen into a bit of state of disrepair you know probably aligned to the managed decline of the rest of the estate.

Grenfell Action Blog.

21st February 2013.[4]

Four years, three months and twenty-three days before the fire.

RABIA. Here is an extract from the most recent Fire Risk Assessment of Grenfell Tower, conducted in November 2012:

MAHER. 'Portable firefighting equipment [...] was out of test date according to the label on the extinguishers. Some located in the roof level areas had "condemned" written on them in large black writing.'

ED. We understood very early that we were never gonna beat the council. They were you know, they were too powerful, RBKC Council were not going to respect us, listen to us, change the way they were, so the blog was like it was a historical document. We weren't gonna win but we sure as hell weren't gonna just let them do what they were doing to us. We wanted to record what was happening to us.

Friday 3rd July 2009.

Seven years, eleven months before the fire.

AUDIO REPORTAGE. A South London block of flats [has been] gutted by a major fire. The blaze ripped through Lakanal House in Camberwell this afternoon [...] It's been confirmed that six people died, three bodies found at the scene included a six-year-old and two adults. The fire which swept through the block on Havel Street trapped thirty people. They have been rescued as more than a hundred firefighters battle to contain the flames.[5]

CAST MEMBER. [*Cast member name*] here. Let me tell you a bit about the Lakanal House fire. It started as a television fire in a single flat, and then the flames burst out of the window. There were new panels under the windows which were combustible so the fire started spreading up and down the building.

After the Great Fire of London they made a rule that you can't use combustible materials on the outside of buildings.

Walk around London and you'll see blocks built after the First World War and they're all concrete, they're all brick, they don't have combustible facades. Some say that's one of the reasons why London survived the Blitz.

CAST MEMBER. I'm [*cast member name*]. In the 1980s, Margaret Thatcher's government changed the existing building regulations. They said they did this to encourage innovation – and it's true the regulations were out of date – but getting rid of the regulations helped the building industry cut costs. What they often called red tape was stopping them using cheaper materials.

The new regulations were worded differently. Instead of saying combustible materials were banned, they said that (*Does air-quotes.*) 'buildings had to adequately resist the spread of flame'.

CAST MEMBER. So the government had gone from telling builders what they were *not* allowed to do, to telling them: 'You work out what to do as long as you don't start a fire.' The government did include something in the new building regulations called Approved Document B – which contained guidance that was meant to help builders know what to do.

CAST MEMBER. When the inquest into the six people who had died at Lakanal House was over, the coroner sent letters to Eric Pickles, who was the Secretary of State of the Department for Communities and Local Government.

She asked him to look at the 'stay put' policy.

CAST MEMBER. 'Stay put' was Britain's gold standard of behaviour in a fire. It meant that unless the fire was in your flat, or very near to it, you could assume that it would be put out before reaching you and so you should stay inside.

CAST MEMBER. Because the people at Lakanal had stayed in their flats, the coroner recommended that the government issue new national guidance on when 'stay put' was to be used.

She also wrote to Eric Pickles about Approved Document B. She recommended that the government rewrite it, especially with reference to the spread of fire over, as she put it, 'the external envelope of the building'.

CAST MEMBER. Which just means the walls.

CAST MEMBER. Approved Document B was so badly worded that the industry either didn't understand it, or could get away with pretending that they didn't. The coroner was effectively warning the government that if they didn't make the wording clearer there might be more fires like Lakanal.

She ended her letter by saying that she thought Eric Pickles' department had the power to take action, and asking him please to tell his department about her recommendations.

On screen:

'20 May 2013.

From the Rt Hon Eric Pickles, Secretary of State for Communities and Local Government now Baron Pickles of Brentwood and Ongar.'

ERIC PICKLES. Dear Coroner,

I have noted your concerns about the difficulties with the interpretation of Approved Document B. I can assure you that my department is committed to a programme of simplification. However, the design of fire protection in buildings is a complex subject and should remain, to some extent, in the realm of professionals. We have commissioned research. We expect this work to form the basis of a formal review leading to the publication of a new edition of the Approved Document B in 2016–17.

CAST MEMBER. It wasn't done by June 2017, the time of the Grenfell Tower fire.

CAST MEMBER. A revolving door of housing ministers including Eric Pickles, Stephen Williams, James Wharton and Gavin Barwell, all kicked the Approved Document B amendments into the long grass before leaving post. The one constant was civil servant Brian Martin whose job it would have been to change the wording of Approved Document B with ministers' approval.

On screen:

'The Grenfell Tower Inquiry started on 14th of September 2017 and ended in November 2022.'

Inquiry space, 29th March 2022.[6]

CAST MEMBER. Brian Martin, Head of Technical Policy in the Technical Policy Division of the Ministry of Housing, Communities and Local Government.

QC. [Mr Martin, in response to the Lakanal House coroner's letter to your minister you wrote] 'we don't plan to do anything. We only have a duty to respond to the coroner, not kiss her backside [...]' This discloses your attitude to the coroner's recommendations, which would not tend to indicate that they were being taken very seriously; do you agree?

BRIAN MARTIN. Clearly it's an informal comment [...] The statutory situation was that under the Coroners Rules – I forget the legislation – the department must respond within a fixed amount of time, but there's no requirement on the department to do what the coroner recommends, that's for the Secretary of State to consider [...]

QC. Did you understand the coroner to be indicating by [her] words that the guidance on external fire spread in Approved Document B, was not clear enough to the reader.

Pause.

BRIAN MARTIN. [...] I can't remember exactly what we were thinking [...] We came to the conclusion that the coroner was referring to [a] previous edition. We'd, in our view at the time, improved that text, and I understand that's a contentious point now, but at that time we thought that text had been improved, and it made sense to do all of this in a single exercise. We didn't see it as being an urgent issue [...]

Inquiry space, 22nd March 2022.

QC. Can we look back at your witness statement [...] You say '[a full technical review of Approved Document B] would have to be set against the Government's priorities of the day, which were deregulation and promoting house building.'

Now, the two deregulatory policies in operation [...] I think were one regulation in, one regulation out, which became one in, two out and then one in, three out, and the Red Tape Challenge?

Was it your understanding throughout that these policies applied to Approved Document B?

BRIAN MARTIN. Yes.

QC. [...] Given that [...] Approved Document B [is] specifically and entirely directed to the protection of life safety and not to the protection of industry or any other economic or commercial interest, what would be wrong with letting somebody [...] who had life safety as their absolute priority craft [...] the approved document?

BRIAN MARTIN. The country would be bankrupt.

QC. Would it?

BRIAN MARTIN. We'd all starve to death, ultimately, I suppose, if you took it to its extreme. I'm not sure that would happen in practice. But that's the policy conundrum that governments are faced with, is you need to balance the cost of regulation with its benefits.

QC. Death by fire or death by starvation, and that's for the government to choose between; is that, in its most extreme form –

BRIAN MARTIN. In its most – I mean, I don't think anyone talked about it in those terms, but that's the principle, and ensuring that – finding the right balance is what governments have to try and do.

QC. Yes. And the balance point, would you accept this, the pivot point, isn't exactly halfway between the two: it would be somewhere between the two as a matter of judgement based on the best information available?

BRIAN MARTIN. Yes. There's a political element to that as well, I guess.

QC. Which is what?

BRIAN MARTIN. Well, in the case of this particular period of time, the government of the day was concerned about the damage to the economy that had occurred as a result of the financial crisis, and so it was focusing on trying to shift that balance so that industry was freer to improve the economy.

QC. And possibly adopt slightly lower, slightly weak standards of fire safety?

BRIAN MARTIN. If you follow that through, yes.

JUDITH. In Kensington and Chelsea the council basically let the Tenants Management Organisation do what it wanted.

The scrutiny was very, very lax. The Tenants Management Organisation board, I think they received, I think they were half-yearly reports on progress against key performance indicators and they always showed that, you know, performance was ninety-six per cent, ninety-three per cent, it was bit like a North Korean election. After the fire when the Lancaster West management was taken back in-house, we discovered that over three thousand, five hundred repairs are still outstanding... quite, you know, I mean quite mindblowing.

There was also a programme of replacement of all the doors across the estate with fire-compliant doors and we got to the point where the housing property scrutiny committee was told, you know, there were only two doors outstanding. After the fire they discovered that, sixty-four per cent of the doors in Grenfell Tower were not fire-compliant.

Eventually the council got money from the extension of leases on Chelsea properties to put towards refurbishing the tower.

The Tenant Management Organisation chose Rydon to do the refurbishment.

Rydon's bid was the lowest of three, but it was still above the sum the Royal Borough of Kensington and Chelsea had made available.

MAHER. The refurbishment was a nightmare. They closed one of the entrances to the building so people had to access the building using a bridge.

It ended up being quite a journey. I kept hurting myself, I had to carry all my own shopping – this was before my wife and children joined me. They promised to open the proper entrance within a fortnight but it took seven months. It got to the point where I'd just wait for any passer-by to come along, and beg them to help me get my shopping up to the flat.

JUDITH. At the first consultation they said 'Well your new heating system will be where your old one is in the kitchen.' No problem, everyone was quite happy with that. Then Rydon were appointed as the contractor. I think they discovered it was going to cost an awful lot more than they had bid for. Then obviously they spoke to the Tenant Management Organisation about the heating units and the TMO said 'Oh yes we quite understand it'll be much easier to put them in the hallway rather than going all the way through to the kitchen.'

ED. We went to the show flats and it was the first time they showed us the new boiler had been positioned in the hallway, it was gas, pipework coming out, destroying our properties.

On screen:

The photo of the pipes to and from the new proposed boiler.[7]

And we turned around to him and sort of said, you know how would you like this in your house? And he turned round to us and said:

MAN. Well if I was getting it for nothing I wouldn't mind.

ED. And to me that kind of sums up the whole of how we were being treated. That was a senior manager from Rydon, you're getting it for nothing, you've got no right to complain. We aren't getting it for nothing, these are our homes. I mean I think you pay the cost of your house a couple of times over if you live there over forty years or something.

BELLAL. They tried to install the boilers next to the electric box right in the middle of the flat. Now we had an issue with that because the door as it is, is narrow, and the corridor is narrow and the boiler would stick out another I don't know four inches, or three or four inches whatever. Now if you are coming in with a pushchair that's a problem.

NICK. I said look, I'm a leaseholder, I want my new boiler where my old boiler is. I said I don't want it in my corridor. I come home one day and my wife, who had Alzheimer's, had been home alone and they'd sent the people to put the pipes in so we had to have it in our corridor.

BELLAL. We have known that with them it's all about cutting costs.

Inquiry space, 15th October 2020.

CAST MEMBER. David Gibson, Tenant Management Organisation's Head of Capital Investment.

QC. Mr Gibson, did it not occur to you that the T[enant] M[anagement] O[rganisation]'s budget was simply too low for the project that you wanted?

DAVID GIBSON. No.

QC. No?

DAVID GIBSON. No.

QC. Why is that?

DAVID GIBSON. We were actually quite pleased when we saw the Rydon tender submission figures because it wasn't as big a gap as we thought there might be, and we thought: this is something that we can make work.

QC. Yet you still wanted them to come down. You realised, presumably, that the Rydon bid was significantly cheaper than the next bid up, wasn't it?

DAVID GIBSON. That's correct.

QC. [...] And now you wanted a further eight hundred thousand pounds taken off. Mr Gibson, my question is: did it not occur to you to [...] say: 'Look, this budget is simply too small for what we want, we need to rethink the scope of our project'?

DAVID GIBSON. No. We thought the gap was bridgeable. We'd already identified some things that would bridge that gap.

Inquiry space, 28th July 2020.

CAST MEMBER. Stephen Blake, Refurbishment Director, Rydon.

QC. Mr Blake, do you accept that [...] Rydon was confident that it could meet the Tenant Management Organisation's target of saving by using aluminium in lieu of zinc for the cladding?

STEPHEN BLAKE. Yes.

Inquiry space, 26th October 2020.

CAST MEMBER. Peter Maddison, Director of Assets and Regeneration at the Royal Borough of Kensington and Chelsea.

QC. Mr Maddison. You were asked by the T[enant] M[anagement] O[rganisation]'s legal advisers: 'Did the Kensington and Chelsea Tenant Management Organisation consider the possibility of this being an abnormally low tender and are you satisfied that Rydon's bid is sustainable?' Did you tell the board the next day that the question was one which had been actually asked?

PETER MADDISON. It had been... I didn't say it had been asked by [our legal advisers] [...] but it had been an issue that had been considered in the original evaluation [...] I understood, so I think consideration was given to this, and in reality the project was delivered on budget, so that's the best sign as to whether or not the price was the correct price.

QC. Well, Mr Maddison, if I may say so, the fact that the project was delivered on budget is not of great assistance to us, given that we know what happened to the building.

Inquiry space, 22nd July 2020.

CAST MEMBER. Simon Lawrence, Rydon's Contract Manager.

QC. You refer in an email [...] to pressure and criticism from the 'rebel residents'. Who were the 'rebel residents', Mr Lawrence?

SIMON LAWRENCE. At the time there was a vocal group of residents that either didn't want the work to proceed or wanted it to proceed in a different way, and things like boilers installed in different areas, and they weren't happy with the T[enant] M[anagement] O[rganisation] and the way the work was progressing [...]

QC. What information had been given to you that allowed you to form the impression that some of the residents were 'rebels', in your words?

SIMON LAWRENCE. I think at that stage there was a group that printed posters, stuck them on their doors, and refused to allow access for the works to be carried out.

TURUFAT. Yeah, I had that poster so don't, 'don't knock don't come'.

BELLAL. With them it's all about saving money. I offered them, I said to him, because I used to do a little bit of underground work, electrician's mate and so on and so forth. I said look all it is, is a matter of extending a conduit through the bathroom round to the back. I told them I will pay actually because I know it's about cutting costs. And they were well if you refuse for us to put, install it in here your, your water and heating is going to be cut off, um which did get me a little bit nervous.

TURUFAT. We used to get a letter that they would take us to court you know. I was very strong about it – I'm a citizen and you know, I work, pay the rent, pay the tax – so you know I have nothing, I haven't done anything wrong.

BELLAL. One of the days I was going down and I was talking to one of them er in the lift and I was having a go at them kind of thing and Ed Daffarn was actually in the lift at the time and he starts having a go at them as well saying:

ED. It's unacceptable what you lot are doing.

BELLAL. And we have a chat after that and I tell my situation and he is like listen he's like:

ED. I've done the same, I haven't, I haven't let them put my boiler in the front. Don't worry about them cutting off your, your water supply, it's against the law. You have young children; they can't cut it off.

BELLAL. So I started to realise that actually I am not on my own.

HANAN. We started a petition to complain about safety and quality issues relating to the refurbishment. As a committee, we went round and knocked on residents' doors to explain the issues and add names to the petition.

I remember Steve Power, bless him. They were threatening him. They said they were going to take him to court. He held out.

ED. They said that we were barraging the council with emails. We were challenging the council, we were trying to hold them to account and holding the Tenant Management Organisation to account, because no one else was. We don't have a right to write emails?

If they could show me one email that was not a valid email, let them do it but they won't be able to because every single email had a purpose.

I'm a social worker yeah you know like if one of my clients doesn't like me, if he feels that I'm interfering in his life that blah, blah, blah, then and wants to kind of you know spit on the floor when I'm near him or not look at me or acting in an aggressive way towards me, it's not my job to discriminate against him and only supply services to the big clients that smile at me. The challenge of my job is to work as effectively with those people as it is with the people that, that engage more readily with me, that's the challenge.

With the council and the councillors, they couldn't understand that they were public servants in a local authority, and that you had a right to challenge them. They just took it personally and would fight back in a personal way. It was disgusting and that goes right from like right from the very top down.

The council helped me greatly in my life, the council paid for me to go to rehab, rehoused me, I've got a lot to thank RBKC for. If they had treated us with respect when we started, none of this would have happened.

TURUFAT. I had my son with a pram and the lift wasn't working and this person helped me, took the pram all the way to seventh floor and you know we had a long chat and we knew about all this meeting but it wasn't convenient for me with my son to go to an evening meeting.

And to be honest with you I am before the refurbishment I was very quiet – but that really hit me there is you know there is another person fighting for us and you know I said I have to involve with that and I start going to the meeting with my son. I am not vocal but the present me being there a was a support.

ED. The reason that a hundred and twenty people from Grenfell Tower attended those meetings is because every single one of them, it wasn't because we told them this is what they needed to do, it was because they felt so aggrieved against the Tenant Management Organisation.

HANAN. Got to a point where, where there were thirty-three of us who literally said no, we're not having the boilers in the hallway, and we're not letting you win. But there were people and you could see how sad they were that they, they felt they'd given in but they were scared. And they were tired. They wear you down with their threats.

RABIA. We held out until the last ones and then they sort of admitted and said fine we will do it for you. I had mine in the kitchen. We are not budging.

NICK. A friend of mine came up and they had a cigarette and they had the window open and I see them drop one little bit of ash on the plastic window ledges and it burnt a hole. I went: Brian, that's brand new and it's never gonna be able to get rid of that, put your cigarette out and I knew from then like wow that's cigarette ash and it made a brown stain.

MAHER. I wasn't as knowledgeable as the builder who was putting in the cladding. But I saw him putting in sponge, silver aluminium, plastic, and I said, 'What on earth are you doing that for?' He said it was insulation, against the cold. I thought to myself at the time that stuff will go up in flames in an instant.

NICK. They told us it was going to be much warmer with new radiators, but it was colder. I bought slippers and pyjamas because there was all the breeze around my ankle.

HANAN. My brother, higher up, you could hear the wind howling.

RABIA. And the windows didn't really lock properly.

BELLAL. If you tried to force it down you could feel the whole bracket trying to come off the window. I called them in, they go to me no, no, no that's standard that's normal they are new windows they will release their self after a while which kind of made sense sometimes these are stiff in the beginning. Months went by and it still didn't fix itself, I called them again. The guy came in, he forced it down: didn't close but it ain't open.

HANAN. My windows broke more than once. It literally came off the hinge and I've got children and not only that, I mean I'm an adult you can lose balance whatever and fall from where we were on the ninth floor. They taught my son Zak who was young, they taught him how to rehinge it. They weren't gonna come and fix it.

TURUFAT. A month before the fire the head of the Tenant Management Organisation and and the head of Rydon came to my flat and we show them you know you just put a candle and you will see how draughty it is. It was terrible really really terrible, terrible, it wasn't fit properly or the size of the window wasn't right. They, they the lady clearly I remember she took a note they acknowledge they knew that there was a problem. They never came back.

Sometimes you wish you have everything recorded but you know the practically life is not like that. It can't be done but yeah yeah we knew, and they knew, that's the saddest part.

HANAN. After they changed the doors, my front door wouldn't close. When I called they did send somebody within four hours but instead of like doing a proper job, he just took the metal pipe out. Same thing happened to my brother. A lot of people – the same thing happen.

NATASHA. [My] door literally just dropped off its hinges. It wasn't very much longer after it had been installed, they were new. And then someone came out and took out the self-closing mechanism that was in the – it was like a chain, kind of quite heavy chain, I think it was, or pole or something, and he took it out.

Once he'd taken it out, the door no longer closed by itself, no longer knocked you out as you left. He said someone would be back to, I assume, replace it, but that never really materialised.[8]

HANAN. [As part of the refurb they converted the two bottom floors into flats. Instead of calling those new floors lower ground, et cetera, they just decided to renumber all our floors so] I was on the sixth floor before the refurbishment, and my brother was on the eighteenth. After the refurb my floor number changed to nine and my brother's to twenty-first.

TURUFAT. And the floor number moved. I started at the fourth and after the refurbishment it ended up at the seventh.

ANTONIO. Before when I got in the lift, I [used to press] seven. After they changed the floor numbers I had to press ten... To confuse us you know.

TURUFAT. It wasn't easy to adjust to that after maybe like twenty years and you haven't moved flat but your floor is changed.

RABIA. The new signs in the stairwell weren't proper signs, the numbers were just stencilled onto the walls.

ED. If you had a visitor to the flat, they would end up getting lost the whole time, because the whole numbering system just didn't make any sense. And if our friends who even had some familiarity with the building would get lost, then what would happen if the firefighters came?

It was just a great example of someone that didn't know the building, didn't know the community, making a decision on our behalf that could have been sorted out in a completely different way. But they didn't live there, they didn't care about us, didn't care about the impact that changing the floor numbers would have on you.[9]

JUDITH. After the refurbishment with the residents I submitted a petition asking for an independent review of how the refurbishment had been carried out. It went to the housing property scrutiny committee, the Tenant Management Organisation obviously attended those meetings and they said: 'Well we'll do our own internal review.' They did an internal review which was so inaccurate as to be unbelievable and for example it said that there were only five complaints and I submitted over twenty myself let alone all the complaints that the residents made.

ED. And of course, they came away with a report that said how brilliantly they'd done. All the residents were happy. It was just a complete stitch-up.

We said at the time it's gonna take a catastrophe here before the council wakes up to what's really going on.

We were told by the council like well who voted for you, who gives you the right to have a voice and I'm like last time I checked this was the UK and we have freedom of speech.

People talk about the Grenfell Action Group being prophets of the fire.

We weren't prophets. The fire was a logical conclusion of a borough council, Royal Borough of Kensington and Chelsea, that was failing to scrutinise a landlord that was failing to implement health and safety. Even when the Fire Brigade were getting involved, the Tenant Management Organisation weren't responding in time to these orders. So yeah, although the horror of what happened could never be imagined, it was just simply unimaginable, it was like, it was a prediction rather than a prophecy.

To predict something is going to happen and have it happen and not be able to stop it: there's no words for that.

TURUFAT. The day before, before the fire it was kind of a relaxing morning for me. I had the day off from work. I took my son to school and his friend mum was with me. We said, 'Oh let's sit down by the café, just have a talk,' so we went to the cafe and we had a chat like, 'That's the mum who lost her son.'

And we're talking about how beautiful the area is, how lucky we are like you know we have the sons together, the gym is there, the swimming lesson is there, they used to have tae kwon do – so, we're saying we're so grateful it's a lovely area how you know how nice people are. And we saw quite a few people from the tower, when I say that quite a few people who lost their life actually on that day, and we had normal conversation with everyone and I think we stayed there for a couple of hours. It was a normal day and a normal evening.

MAHER. We were about to celebrate our twenty-seventh wedding anniversary, my wife and I, on the 15th of June.

We decided to invite our friends from the building.

[We shopped for the meal. We were going to cook] Kabsa – rice with chicken. And tabbouleh and kibba. And salad, and some juice, and we were going to bring cake.

We watched TV, we prayed the Isha prayer, then my wife and I went to sleep.

RABIA. I remember going to Argos to buy a new house phone. I remember my son was sick. And my car got clamped. I was upset about that, cos that day my mother-in-law was back from Morocco and, we had plans to go and see her.

I remember speaking to my mom about my son being sick, and she said, 'Oh, you're on your own.' Bellal was away. She said, 'Why don't you come spend the night with me?' And I didn't want to go. So I ended up staying at home.

It was just me and the kids. I went to bed, I wasn't going to fast the next day because I wasn't feeling well cos I was pregnant. I went to bed.

NATASHA. I work for the Waitrose arm of John Lewis. I'm a manager. Come home from work as I do normally. Um, fell asleep on the sofa as I did most nights.

HANAN. I went to work, I'm a teacher as usual on Tuesday, 13th of June 2017. It was Ramadan, so I was fasting. After I left school, I bumped into my brother Abdulaziz, my sister-in-law Faouzia, and my nephews Yasin and Mehdi. I gave

my brother a kiss on the cheek. Abdulaziz said they were on
their way to buy water and kill time until the sun set and they
could have their iftar food. I told him that I was going home
to cook and he shook his head and gave me a teasing look as
if to say he was sorry for me with so much on my plate, as
I was there cooking, looking after the kids and I had a full-
time job. In our culture, this isn't the norm for women.

By the time I got upstairs to our flat, Faouzia was ringing me
saying Abdulaziz had said that I shouldn't cook, and should
go to their place for dinner that night instead. I said I would
have loved to do that but I had guests coming so I couldn't.
If I hadn't had guests coming, I would have been with them
in their flat that night.[10]

ANTONIO. On the 13th of June I was in Italy. I came back.
I flew from Venice to London Gatwick. I got to the tower
around seven o'clock.

My son Christopher was working and I called him,
Christopher, I'm back. It was a nice warm evening,
I remember. So, around nine, ten o'clock, ten-thirty, I went
to bed. Ten-thirty, I went to bed.

TIAGO. My mum's cousin had come to visit from South Africa.
We talked about a load of different things until my cousins
needed to go. My parents said: 'We'll take you,' and they all
left. I went to watch a TV show on my computer.

NICK. My wife was asleep on the sofa um I was asleep on the
floor I had a DVD in that I was just um I fell asleep on the
floor beside my dog.

ED. I recently started listening to a radio show, Duncan Barkes
on Radio London and that show finished at one o'clock in
the morning, so if I hadn't been listening to him, I may have
gone to bed a bit earlier, I don't know what would have
happened.

UNIT 16: The first call.[11]

00:54:29.

Sound of ringing which is then cut off.

OPERATOR. Fire Brigade.

CALLER. Yeah, hello, hi. In the fire is flat sixteen, Grenfell Tower.

OPERATOR. Sorry, a fire where?

CALLER. Flat sixteen, Grenfell Tower. In the fridge.

OPERATOR. Right, hang on.

CALLER. Flat sixteen, Grenfell Tower.

OPERATOR. Flat sixteen. And what's the postcode?

CALLER. W11 1TG.

OPERATOR. W11, 1, T for Tango?

CALLER. Yeah, but coming quick, please.

OPERATOR. Yeah, would you just – I have to get the address, okay. Glen–

CALLER. Flat sixteen, Grenfell Tower, W11 1TG.

OPERATOR. The Fire Brigade are on their way. Are you outside?

CALLER. Yes, yes. I'm outside.

CAST MEMBER. We're going to take a short break. Please feel free to stay here, or go out for some air and something to drink if you want. We'll see you after the break.

ACT TWO

On screen:

'14th June 2016.'

Continuation of the 999 calls that ended Act One.

Recorded call playback:

BELHAILU KEBEDE. Quick, quick, quick.

CRO (CONTROL ROOM OFFICER). They're on their way already.

BELHAILU KEBEDE. It's burning.

CRO. Yes, I know it's burning but they are on their way. You've only just called. As long as you're okay, yeah.

BELHAILU KEBEDE. Okay.

CRO. Just tell me how many floors you've got there?

BELHAILU KEBEDE. It's the fourth floor.

CRO. Right, okay. Okay, so the fire engines are on the way, they will be there, soon, okay?

BELHAILU KEBEDE. Okay.

CRO. You've only just called us so it will take a minute for them to get there.

BELHAILU KEBEDE. Yes, yes.

End of recorded call.

CM (Crew Manager) Jamal Stern, Kensington.[12]

CM JAMAL STERN. All the lights came on, our mobilisation system kicked in saying 'Mobilise, mobilise' informing us there is a shout […] We all went and made our way down to the appliance.

TIAGO. I was watching *The Expanse* on my computer, so a friend of mine had suggested me to watch it, to be honest to this day I haven't finished watching that episode.

Suddenly the door smacked the wall, it smacked the doorstopper. It was my dad.

When he was on his way back from dropping my cousins, the lift door had opened on the fourth floor and he had seen smoke.

The only person to ever tell never to open the door loudly like that would be my dad. So I stood up and I was like 'What happened?'

And my dad seemed like he was a bit out of breath and he just says, 'Get dressed you are going downstairs I think there is a fire.'

CM JAMAL STERN. We made our way to the entrance [...] I saw this fire trickling out of just that one window as I was walking past [...] There were no alarm bells for me [...] It just confirmed that there was a fire there [...] The only thing that was a bit out of the ordinary was the smoke coming out of what looked like vents in the building but at that time hindsight, it didn't really, I didn't pick up on it.

TIAGO. I was thinking that the fire was just going to be dealt with. Because you know the 'stay put' policy was always drilled into my head.

My father he knew about 'stay put', he just, you know, he just felt more secure being outside. He has always trusted his instincts above anything else. Me on the other hand, I've always put my trust in science and regulations. I'm not the kind of person who is, like I'm not anti-establishment. Even at school, I was always the kind of person who always followed the rules and I would always assume that all regulations are based on some sort of science. To be, be perfectly honest I would have stayed put.

CM JAMAL STERN. The [inside] staircase seems quite tight spiralled with landings, you would struggle getting two people walking shoulder to shoulder up them [...] There was no signs of smoke, could hear nothing there was no signs of panic from anyone. When we got to the fourth floor, we opened the door, there wasn't much smoke in the lobby area, we noticed that crews had been committed into the fire flat.

TIAGO. So it was almost like I was put between a rock and a hard place in terms of, should I follow what the policy states or should I follow what my dad states? But he was the person right there and you know, if I wanted to have an argument with him later, I would have it with him later.

I was wearing my pyjamas. Put on my trousers. It was actually these trousers that I left with. My keys and my wallet were in my pocket already. I left my computer on, I didn't pick up any of my valuables. We even locked the door. It was that level of trust that we would be back by the end of the evening.

01:13:19.

RADIO COMMS. M2FN Golf 331 from WM O'Keeffe make pumps six request one TL, sorry, HP, Golf 331, over.

RADIO COMMS. Make pumps six and one HP received.

NATASHA (*eleventh floor*). I was woken up by the sound of sirens. Took absolutely no notice, got up off the sofa. My partner was on the sofa still watching the TV. I walked to bed. Got in bed, went back to sleep.

ED (*sixteenth floor*). I'm lying in bed, I heard my neighbour, one-three-five, smoke alarm going bing, bing, bing.

I didn't even bother getting out of bed, I just lay in bed thinking my next-door neighbour's burnt some food or something like that. It wasn't that unusual for a smoke alarm to go off even at that time in the morning.

HANAN (*ninth floor*). After I had fallen asleep, my husband Salah got up to go to the toilet and I heard him call my name. I remember waking up and smelling smoke and plastic.[13]

BELLAL. I was away from home. I had called Rabia at around twelve-thirty and we chatted for about thirty to forty-five minutes until Rabia said:

RABIA. There's something going on, I can hear sirens.

BELLAL. We didn't think much of it because there had been fires in flats before and it was contained. But then she said she could see smoke coming past the kitchen window, quite a lot of smoke. I told her to call the Fire Brigade just for reassurance. After she got off the phone I told her that she would be fine, but just in case she should wake the kids.

NATASHA. I was woken by voices on the landing. All my neighbours are really good neighbours, um, so to hear voices on the landing was really unusual. So, my bedroom is right by the front door. Um, so, I got up and opened the door, looked round and I could see my neighbours from across the way. And their English was not very good and they were saying, 'Smoke, smoke, fire.' And I remember looking at the lifts and seeing that one of them was out of service and one was still in service. I could see a tiny bit of smoke in the corner, but nothing. So, I was like, okay, I said you guys, you go. That was exactly what I said, and I shut the door.

HANAN. My husband was adamant that the procedure was that we were to stay put but my son Zak said, 'We are not doing that Mum we are getting out.' He was sixteen and he just took on the parent role and I just felt like I was a child. He left the flat to see whether the landing on our floor was okay. Then he ran back into his sister's bedroom, who was eight at the time, and emerged carrying her and said, 'I'm going.' He left.

01:19:08.

RADIO COMMS. M2FN Golf 272, make pumps eight, over.

HANAN. I could see ash in the kitchen blowing in from the window, and the smoke was getting thicker. I put a brown robe and brown headscarf on and I pushed my feet into a pair of Crocs. Salah put his work clothes on, a navy-blue T-shirt and denim jeans. Then we left the flat.

ED. I heard a bit of shouting out in the hallway, I can't remember if it was 'fire, fire' or if it was just a commotion and that wasn't normal.

HANAN. On the fourth floor I saw two firefighters on the stairs. I froze, thinking that they were going to tell me to go back to the flat and 'stay put'. And the firefighter who was kneeling was in the way. Then, he adjusted himself slightly, which gave me just enough space to jump over his foot. I kept running down all the way down. The CCTV image has me leaving the building at one-twenty-one a.m.

ED. So, we're looking at like quarter past, twenty past one in the morning, shouting out in the hallway. Enough to get me out of bed.

Inquiry space, 19th July 2018.

CAST MEMBER. Crew Manager Jamal Stern.

QC. You say at the top of page nine of your witness statement: 'Large smoke was reported on the sixth [...] I made my way up to the sixth to have a look. The sixth-floor lobby was quite heavy smoke-logged. It was low, it was enough for me to make a safe approach to the flat. My initial thoughts were maybe the fire had jumped, maybe there was a window opened, and it had actually breached into sixth-floor flat [...] I checked the door [...] It wasn't hot with the back of my hand. It was closed but unlocked so I opened it and had a quick peek, it was heavily smoke-logged' [...]

Did you call out inside the flat to see if anybody was inside?

CM JAMAL STERN. No.

QC. Do you remember whether you told anybody on that floor to run?

CM JAMAL STERN. No.

QC. Could you describe the smoke?

CM JAMAL STERN. It was thick black smoke, floor to ceiling.

QC. Did you have any thoughts about whether you needed to be telling residents on the sixth floor that you'd just arrived on to leave the building?

CM JAMAL STERN. My initial thoughts was just to get firefighters with equipment up to those flats.

01:24:09.

RADIO COMMS. M2FN Golf 271, make pumps ten, over.

Inquiry space, 25th June 2018.

WM (Watch Manager) Michael Dowden.

QC (*to* WM MIKE DOWDEN). As a watch manager, would you expect to be incident commander if you were first at the scene? [...]

WM MIKE DOWDEN.Yes. Generally for watch manager at the scene, your role sort of, in terms of command, would go up to four pumps.

QC. So, we're now at 01:24 and we've gone from six pumps to ten pumps in eleven minutes or so [...] Was that an increase in demand for appliances that you had ever experienced before?

WM MIKE DOWDEN. Not at that time, at that short timescale, no [...] It's something that I, as an incident commander, have never witnessed before [...]

QC. You would normally expect a deputy assistant commissioner to take over incident command at ten pumps, I think.

WM MIKE DOWDEN. That's correct.

QC. And he would have an assistant commissioner as a monitoring officer at that level of pumps.

WM MIKE DOWDEN. Correct.

QC. So is it right that [...] you should've had much more senior support on the ground and, in fact, shouldn't have had incident command at all, according to normal procedures?

WM MIKE DOWDEN. In procedures and in normal expected circumstances, and I think that just lends – tells the story of how unprecedented this event was, how quick the external envelope of that building was compromised, the way that fire just – I say it was relentless.

QC. As at June 14th, were you aware that the LFB had written to a number of London councils saying that external fire spread on high-rise residential buildings as a result of being clad in combustible panels presented a generic health and safety issue? Did you know that?

WM MIKE DOWDEN. I remember seeing some – not internally in the LFB but in the local press, in a newspaper – about a letter that had been sent to Hammersmith and Fulham Council, I believe […] But not something that was sent out internally within the London Fire Brigade, no.

QC. Right. So, could we say that your knowledge was as good as the person in the street about that letter?

WM MIKE DOWDEN. Yes, I would say so […]

HANAN. In the time that it had taken me to go downstairs, the fire had flown up to the seventeenth floor of the building.[14]

   01:27:26.

RADIO COMMS. Further traffic, make pumps fifteen, over.

HANAN. I called my brother, Abdulaziz. He said he was aware of something going on, and he kept saying, 'Shall I come down? What do you think?' I said, 'I think you should get out,' and told him, 'It's on my side now not on your side.' He said, 'Alright sis I'm coming.'

MAHER. My eldest daughter knocked on our bedroom door. [*Long pause.*] She knocked. She said: 'Dad, there's a fire.' She said they were going to go downstairs. I said no, wait here. I opened the front door, and realised there was smoke coming up, black. I closed the door and said: 'Clearly there's something going on – a fire in a room or a flat – just stay here.' My eldest daughter said 'No, we need to go downstairs.' My youngest said – 'Touch the wall, Dad, it's like fire' – the wall next to their bed, in the living room.

I said, 'You go downstairs, all of you.' My wife refused, saying that with my condition I needed help. I said 'No, the kids are here. Go downstairs because you'll get down fast, but I'm slow. Go – if they lose me, at least they'll have you.' [*Long sigh.*] I made my wife and children leave first, because I move slowly.

01:29:46.

RADIO COMMS. M2FN Golf 271, make pumps twenty and FRUs two, over.

HANAN. I called my brother at about one-thirty a.m., and he said, 'I tried [to leave] but I couldn't because there was too much black smoke and we can't see, we can't breathe.' He said, 'It's going to be alright sis isn't it? It's going to be alright?'

BELLAL. The BBC news popped up. I could see live footage of the fire. It was hard to register that it was our home, that this was our building on the TV, covered in fire, and it was the same place my wife and kids were. I was horrified. And it was worse because I couldn't get there.

00:01:21.

RABIA. I'm scared and I've got three young kids and I'm pregnant, I don't know what to do [...]

CRO GOTTS. What, what floor are you on?

RABIA. On the eighteenth floor. We need to get out [...]

CRO GOTTS. Okay, yeah. The fire's on the fourth [...]

RABIA. Are we safe?

CRO GOTTS. I, I obviously can't, erm, I don't, I don't know, I mean, if, if you can get to the window and get some air.

RABIA. There's no smoke in my house yet but – but I tried to get out to go through the fire escape and there's just thick black smoke I'm on the eighteenth. Please send someone [...]

CRO GOTTS. Okay, I'll let them know you're there, okay?

RABIA. All right, okay.

CRO GOTTS. All right, thank you, bye.

AOM (ASSISTANT OPERATIONS MANAGER) NORMAN. Between 01:20 and two-ish all hell broke loose in the control room.[15]

01:25:16.

MAN 1. I'm on the fourteenth floor, it's right on – it's coming past my window.[16]

AOM NORMAN. Right, the fire's actually on the fourteenth floor.

MAN 1. It's on the fourteenth?

AOM NORMAN. No, it's on the fourth, one, two, three, four.

MAN 1. Well, I'm on – fourteen […]

AOM NORMAN. What flat number are – what number are you? One-one-four?

MAN 1. No, I'm one-one-one, I'm on the fourteenth floor, Grenfell Tower, love […]

01:26:58.

WOMAN 1. We're living on the twelfth floor […] My neighbour she's saying the fire in her kitchen already.

CRO FOX. It's at flat sixteen in the Grenfell Towers.

WOMAN 1. No, no, no, we're on the floor twelfth, twelfth.

CRO FOX. Yeah, but I'm telling you – listen, I'm just telling you where the actual fire –

WOMAN 1 (*overspeaking*). But it already come to twelfth.

CRO FOX (*overspeaking*). Is, okay, so, it's flat sixeen.[17]

01:30:00.

WOMAN 3. There's smoke everywhere. You need to get right to the top. The fire's in our house and I'm on the twenty-second floor, everyone's on the twenty-third.

CRO DUDDY. Okay, the fire's on the fifth floor so you're well away from the fire okay?

01:30:38.

WOMAN 1. Our neighbour told us it's actually from their kitchen.

CRO GOTTS. Oh, I see. Okay. Yeah, well we are there and I'll let them know you're on the twentieth but you've just got some smoke up. You're okay though, yeah?

WOMAN 1. Yeah we're still, we are in the neighbours' house.

CRO GOTTS. Oh, okay. All right. Well, it is on the twentieth – you're on the twentieth; it's on the fourth.

HANAN. There was a difference to the way the control room treated people.

I've listened to the nine-nine-nine calls that my brother and his family made that night and I listened to other nine-nine-nine calls and one of the call operators, who was on the phone to my brother also spoke to another man. I've heard this call because it was played in the Inquiry.

This man was next door to my brother and the same operator who got him and his family out and stayed on the phone with him when they did this, this same operator spoke to my family and the response was different. My brother had an accent, the other man didn't.

Obviously my brother was panicking, as you can imagine, and he was told to basically, basically be quiet. And he apologised. My brother apologised. Because he knew that had he not apologised they would not be willing to continue the conversation with him. The operator was like, you know, 'Stop now, calm down, calm down.' I mean… it wasn't polite the way they spoke to my brother. In Grenfell Tower when that was happening.

HANAN. I called my brother's phone back for the third time. Faouzia picked up. I said to her, 'The fire is at top of the building now. You need to get out.' I could hear Abdulaziz talking in the background to the emergency services. Faouzia said the emergency services had said they were coming to rescue them. She sounded calm; I knew she was holding it together for her kids.

I took a video on my telephone at one-thirty-two a.m. In the video, you can see the kitchen light in Abdulaziz's flat go off.

Inquiry space, 12th September 2018.

CAST MEMBER. Acting Control Room Operations Manager Norman.

QC. Okay [...] at twenty-five pumps, 01:30, 01:48 – did you expect to receive more information from the incident ground than just the one informative message that we saw at about 01:16?

AOM NORMAN. I was expecting something, yes.

QC. Did you seek to contact the incident ground for more information about what was going on?

AOM NORMAN. No, I didn't. We were extremely busy in the control room and just didn't have an opportunity, to be honest [...] We would normally chase them after about half an hour to an hour, not after sort of fifteen, twenty minutes [...]

QC. Was there a television link in place? [...]

AOM NORMAN. There was a TV, [...] yes. I think it was working, it just wasn't switched on [...]

QC. Is there a reason for that?

AOM NORMAN. Yes. So, there were two TVs in the control room. There was a large one, forty-five-inch possibly, which has always been there, which I am aware was not working [...] and there was a small one [...] and it was behind the supervisor's desk, so we wouldn't have been able to view it because it was behind us [...] So, I felt early on there was no point in putting it on [...]

QC. Would it have helped to have that television on?

AOM NORMAN. I don't think in the early hours it would've even been on, would it, really?

QC. The first recorded images of the fire taken by the Press Association and recorded by the BBC are timed at 01:30:17. It is therefore likely that if the television had been on, it would have enabled the control room operators to understand better the situation in which they were placed and would have helped them to give accurate and realistic advice to callers, at least in the early stages of the fire.[18]

MAHER. My wife and daughter, when they got down, they spoke to the firefighters, and said, 'My husband is disabled' – my wife was crying, she said – 'My husband is still upstairs, on the ninth floor, here's the flat number, number sixty-four.'

They even wrote on the wall the number of the flat where I was. My daughter wrote sixty-four on the wall. With a pen. It's written on the wall, to this day.

TURUFAT. A telephone call wake up my husband, his phone was on silent but vibrate. I think the person called him quite a few times. He said 'Somebody must be in need.' Our neighbour on the eighteenth floor who phoned he told my husband that there is a fire in the building so my husband hung up and said 'Let's go out.' I had on my pyjama my husband slept with his shorts so he came out with shorts but I needed to put my jogging pants and tracksuit cos you know. I'm a woman I can't go in the middle of the night with my shorts.

I locked the flat behind us. My husband carried my son and we start going. We can see a very, very faint smoke but still it didn't hit us because our focus is just to go out. When we reached to the fifth floor I just saw this very like thick black smoke is like like coming through to your face. I just ran back.

Because I've already started going backward my husband followed me.

And then I start panicking. Real panic. I even said to my husband you know 'What do we do? We have to jump out?' you know and just you know thinking where we gonna land, we know it's we're not safe so I called nine-nine and I told them that we are in on this floor which is the seventh floor up and I told them we try to come and she said 'Okay we are aware of the situation just stay there, you know, they will get you.'

CAST MEMBER. We told you that they put cladding on the building. The cladding they use was Reynobond 55 PE, made by Arconic. The panels were sold flat but they could be bent into cassettes. They used cassettes for Grenfell because they were more attractive and easier to hang. But this made them even more flammable.

Inquiry space, 18th February 2021.

CAST MEMBER. Claude Schmidt, President of Arconic.

QC. Let's look at this email to Claude Wehrle […] from Maxime Bauer of the certification company CSTB.

Claude Wehrle, Manager of Arconic's Technical Sales Support Team, had refused to attend the Inquiry.

The title is, 'Reaction to fire tests on the cassette version' […] It reads:

'Hello Mr Wehrle, we have performed a test on your reference Reynobond PE [cassette cladding]. Unfortunately, we stopped the test before the end […] Note: Fall of large pieces, […] widespread fire on the surface reaching critical values, resulting in the termination of the ongoing test. Therefore, we cannot provide you with a classification for the cassette version' […]

So […] it looks as if the test for PE cassette [cladding] was stopped before the test had been concluded; do you agree?

CLAUDE SCHMIDT (*interpreted*). Oui. (Yes.) […][19]

QC. Can we now go, please […] to an email from Claude Wehrle to others in Arconic […] He says: 'Oops… The performance and classification of Reynobond PE cassette [cladding] following the test this morning is… "F"!!!' […]

Then [his report about] 'Next steps', says: 'For the moment, even if we know that PE material in cassette has a bad behaviour exposed to fire, we can still work in countries with national regulations which are not as restrictive' […] Now, going back into […] Claude Wehrle's witness statement […] he says: 'The intention was for customers […] to be informed of the position when asking about the fire performance of the cassette variant of the product' […]

It looks from that as if Claude Wehrle is saying Arconic's intention was to tell customers about the performance of PE, the classification of PE, only if they asked. Is that correct?

CLAUDE SCHMIDT (*interpreted*). C'est ce qui est écrit là. (That's what is written there.) […]

QC. Do you agree that the classification was significant and important information for customers to know?

CLAUDE SCHMIDT (*interpreted*). Oui. (Yes.) [...]

QC. Mr Schmidt, do you accept that it was a dangerous practice to leave it to the customer [...] to find out rather than volunteering that information?

CLAUDE SCHMIDT (*interpreted*). C'était risqué. (It was risky.)

TIAGO. I was outside just staring at the flames. I had learned that the colour of the flame determines how hot it is. For example, the hotter the flame is, the closer it is to blue or white. So that, you know that again, this was just kind of like rushing through my head. And I just remember being in the Year 8 chemistry lesson just remembering my chemistry teacher saying, okay, fine, roughly what is the temperature of this fire? Let's focus on the science of this whole, of this whole disaster. I was just trying to be completely analytical. Almost like distance myself from what was actually going on.

The fire reaches the top. At this point, I told my sister, let's go to our friend's house. Our friends have a direct view of our own apartment.

RABIA. All the phone calls started from families because they were all local, my phone didn't stop ringing, calling me saying, get out, get out. I said er I said but the firemen said stay.

BELLAL. They had two phones between them. Rabia had her own and Naila had hers. There was a flurry of calls happening between me and Rabia and others.

RABIA. I was getting a bit panicky then thinking, okay, I don't know what's going on, then I had a bang on the door. It was my neighbour. She is saying to me, 'There's a fire, get out, get the kids and get out!'

I told them, no I have spoke to the firemen they said stay you are fine where you are, stay put. My neighbour left and I saw him walk down the stairs as he went from the door I saw like smoke, a lot of smoke. I started panicking think okay how am I gonna, even if I wanted to, the smoke, I don't know

I was oblivious, I didn't know the stairs you know the kids and stuff.

NICK. I was woken by a loud banging at my door. It was just BANG, BANG, BANG.[20] When I opened the front door black smoke just come billowing in. Oh, it was quite frightening, but I was quite cool. And then um then the phone calls started coming because my friend's a fireman and the first one I got, he said: 'There's a big fire in the tower. You need to leave now.' The panic in his voice and you know – 'Get out!' I couldn't carry my wife down forty, you know, forty-six flights of stairs. I got her dressed and then it's like a phone call like:

'Get out your bedroom now because the fire's coming across.'

And we're on the nineteenth floor.

'Get out of your living room go in the kitchen.'

Next thing we just um we're just trapped in our bathroom. You could hear noises being the sirens you don't know the scope of what's going on outside or how this is happening. Is it coming in from next door, is it come in through the front door, is it coming from you, you just don't know and you think if I'm the bathroom I've got water there just put the shower on it's not gonna.

You know Pily was very calm. But um I knew that that smoke that was outside that we wouldn't have made it down if I took her and I couldn't leave her, so I had to make that decision that we were staying together.

ED. I threw on a pair of shorts, T-shirt, went to my front door expecting to open it to find my neighbour outside going shit, I burnt me dinner or whatever and then I opened the door literally a fraction. Just this wave of smoke just came. Like I literally just closed the door and at that moment my heart sort of sunk.

It was like my god, this isn't my neighbour, this is a proper fire, it was like real, not kind of like, fuck and then literally while I was still standing at the door my phone rang and it was one of neighbours from downstairs and he shouted, 'Get out. Get the fuck out.'

There was something about the way he said it that I didn't say look I've opened my front door, there's a lot of smoke out there, there's a 'stay put' policy, I think I'll just wait in my flat. Without kind of consciously thinking I kind of like made my mind up, I'm going, I'm going to get out of here.

NATASHA. Walked back into the bedroom put on my tr... started to put on my trousers and shouted through down to partner and said what's going on outside? And then he must have got up and had a look.

I could see by his reaction, his face that – you know, I trusted him – there's something seriously wrong out there.

ANTONIO. On the way back from work my son Christopher he went for a drink. On the way back in the minicab and he saw a lot of, um, um, ah, Fire, Fire Brigade lorries, he arrived to the tower and he saw the beast burning. He called me:

'Pappi, Pappi, get the fuck out of there, the tower is burning.'

I put down the phone and I opened the, the, the window. People shouting, 'Get out, get out!'

I got dressed and I tried to get out with my rucksack and my everything. I opened the door a little so much smoke came in and, ah, you know, burning. Black, pitch black. Hot and horrible smell, horrible. And so what is going on here, my god.

So, then I said, okay, I went to the bathroom, I, um, ah, rinsed my eyes and then Christopher sent me a photo, which is there, with the tower burning, and I said, my god, look at this, it's unbelievable.

NATASHA. The Fire Brigade still pretty much saying stay where you are, we're gonna come and get you, you know. And I'll be completely honest, I had no reason to distrust them.

ANTONIO. I was picturing myself, okay, if you go out there, um, it's very dark, it's you cannot breathe, you cannot, um, you don't know where you're walking. The fire stair is quite narrow. So, I said, you know, if you lose balance, if you, if you trip over something, if you, if you, if you cannot hold your breathing and you have ten floors to go, what are you gonna do?

And I said, no, I'm not going out. I realised it was very, very, very se– this time it's very serious and, ah, and this one it's not something that happens to other… now it's happening to me.

MAHER. I waited five minutes next to my front door to see if someone would come and help me. There was more smoke coming, and so I decided to use the stairs like everyone else, thinking that maybe while I was going down the stairs, someone would help me. I was horrified to see that the residents were running. At lightning speed.

ANTONIO. The first call that Christopher did, he was crying as well, because he was like, he was like, ah, saying sorry for things that he, you know, if he upset me or so, you know, he was very he thought it was, he thought it was, um, I was in extreme danger, yeah. But I said, Christopher, listen, it's not my day. Keep focused. I need you to keep in touch with the Fire Brigade and to let me know what is going on.

NATASHA. So now, we're now watching what's going on outside. See Fire Brigade shooting the water up this way. And it's really odd. It, it was one of those things that over the years, I suppose, stuff's happened downstairs, and I've stood at the window and watched it. Whether it be police raiding a house or whatever you. I'm that nosey neighbour, ooh what's going on down there. I've always been like this. It was kind of a little bit like that even though I knew it was serious. And I'm taking phone calls from people and all I kept saying to anyone that called is, where is it now?

MAHER. I used my crutches like this. (*Demonstrates*.) I'd put one foot and a crutch here, then the other crutch here, then my left foot, then my right. So I'd go very slowly, bit by bit. I would try to hang on to the banisters, so that nobody would bump into me and I wouldn't fall over. Nobody stopped for me. Nobody helped me.

TIAGO. Me and my sister were watching the real fire and the fire on TV. It was so strange. You know, if people think about your own houses, imagine it being live on TV and literally it's almost like, you turn to the window, you turn to the TV, and it's pretty much the same. You are watching the exact same things.

ED. I go the bathroom, I literally just pulled a towel out, threw it in the sink, run some water so it was wet, wrapped it around my face and then I had, in my back pocket I had my Oyster card and bank cards in a wallet, an Oyster wallet, I had my keys and my phone on the side where I always kept them when I came into the flat or maybe I had my phone in my pocket by that stage because of speaking with my neighbour.

Inquiry space, 19th July 2018.

QC. Was there any difficulty in identifying what floor you were on?

CM JAMAL STERN. There were no numbers in the stairwell, so the only way to check is to hopefully see the numbers on the lift lobby.

QC. The difficulties you had with identifying which floor you were on, did that get in the way of your firefighting operations generally?

CM JAMAL STERN. Yeah, it made it difficult for me myself to know what floor I was on [...]

I was in the stairwell, I turned around and a young man who I now know his name was Sam from the sixteenth floor [...] [said] his dad was bedridden, and he was trapped on the sixteenth floor and he needed help to get him out. At that point, it didn't enter my mind that it was a rescue [...][21]

Because we have a 'stay put' policy that if they're safe, twelve floors above a fire flat, we wouldn't even think about bringing them out of their flat. We'll go up and reassure them, make sure that they are safe and leave them there [...] My anticipation would be that there would be no smoke above the sixth floor.

ED. I opened the door, I turned around, closed the door because that's what you do in a fire and then I kind of turned around and realised that I couldn't see a thing, it was like absolutely pitch black. I couldn't see further than my nose.

CM JAMAL STERN. The sixteenth floor was smoke-logged floor to ceiling, thick black smoke [...] It shocked me. We're floors above the fire floor, with the lobby being smoke-logged

at that density, at that speed, I couldn't rationalise it. It made
no sense to me. You would expect those kinds of conditions
to be – the thick black smoke to kind of present something we
call backdraft conditions, where the compartment is oxygen-
deprived so the smoke gets really thick. And it should be
really hot; it wasn't hot, it was just extremely thick
smoke […] I just couldn't explain it.[22]

ED. I had to get whatever it was, fifteen feet, five metres, out
and diagonally across the hallway to reach the emergency
exit.

Of course, I don't really remember what happened, but
I went towards where I thought the emergency exit was and
didn't find it.

What I found was a wall and then I started pawing against
the wall and instead of working out that wasn't the door, this
was a wall, I need to move, I just started panicking and then
I let go of the towel with my other hand, so my towel fell
down and I was using both my hands to push at this wall and
then I started inhaling the smoke and I actually thought to
myself, this is it.

At that moment a fireman came through the emergency door
and I thought he touched my leg. I was really close to the
emergency exit. The only reason that the fireman was there
was because my neighbour had gone downstairs, had been
unable to persuade his dad to leave the flat and had gone
downstairs and begged the fireman to come up and get his
dad out so that was the only reason that the fireman was
where he was. There weren't like firemen on every landing
getting people out.

CM JAMAL STERN. I stood him up.

ED. I remember them kind of touching my leg and me looking
down and then what I noticed was the smoke was thinner on
the ground, again if my fire safety had been better, I might
have worked out that I needed to crawl along the ground, but
I hadn't done, it was so full of smoke anyway.

CM JAMAL STERN. I stepped back, and guided him out […]
I didn't need to carry the casualty; he stood up and walked.

ED. I got into the stairwell and I just got my head around what was happening. At that stage I don't really remember much smoke in the stairwell, all I can remember is that idea of fight-or-flight coming into operation.

I just ran for my life, I just ran as quick as I could down them stairs and out.

01:35:13, Ed leaves the building.

TURUFAT. After probably five to ten minutes our door knocked like a big bang bang and we open and there is a fireman.

FIREFIGHTER. You have to leave the building.

TURUFAT. We can't, we tried but fourth floor –

FIREFIGHTER. You have to leave.

TURUFAT. What about my son?

FIREFIGHTER. You have to leave.

TURUFAT. And he just turned his face. Only thing I could think of was of what you know if that smoke choked my son. I just grabbed him a water, you know the filter bottle so I had that in my hand and my husband got a scarf to cover our son nose and and again for the second time I locked the door – hoping we come back.

I don't know how we managed to get to downstairs.

MAHER. When I tried to go faster, I fell over. Maybe my crutches fell, maybe I got tired. I hurt my lower back. But I didn't feel – I was rushing to save my life – I didn't feel the pain. Not right away. I just wanted to get out alive. And make sure my children and wife were okay.

TURUFAT. The hardest was fourth floor there was a couple of fireman on that one trying to you know do something with the hose and then that's it when we land to to the ground and we just turn our face and that side of the building was completely on flame.

01:40:48, Turufat leaves the building.

01:43:19.

NATASHA. I'm ringing from Grenfell Tower. I know you know, but there's smoke coming in my house now – Yeah, we've blocked the bottom of the door, yeah we've done all that

ED. I can't really talk about my first sight of the building. Someone came up and I was crying my eyes out.

We were gradually being moved further and further away by the police, the flames were going like right up the side of the building and it was like people at the windows and it was like, it was just fucking so traumatic, it was just, you know. I was like wailing from inside my soul, it was just so distressing. Then the police sort of started moving us away a little a bit and then further away and there was a mixture of residents and onlookers and the police were like not helping us, they weren't like: survivors over here, onlookers over there. They were just like fucking: 'Get back, get back.' I still had a wet towel around me, and I was in fucking trauma. There was a mixture of onlookers, residents and then fucking riot squad ran past us, like all these policemen dressed up in riot gear, it was like, you know. And then this ambulance worker, she leant out of the ambulance shouted at us to go home.

TURUFAT. My husband keep calling those family on the eighteenth floor 'you have to come out' but but again you know they've been told 'stay there, we will get you' who do you, who do you, who do you listen to that time?

MAHER. When I got down to the lobby at the entrance, there were two firefighters. I got to the very last step, and they asked, 'Do you need any help?' I said, 'Now you want to help me?'

01:45, Maher leaves the building.

Inquiry space, 8th September 2020.

CAST MEMBER. Ray Bailey, Harley Curtain Wall, hired by Rydon the builders to put up the cladding and insulation.

QC. [...] Would you have considered the fire performance of the [insulation] being used?

RAY BAILEY. [It] [...] was a new product to us. Daniel spoke to Celotex, had the technical sales manager in, we sent them key drawings and they've signed off on it. So as far as we were concerned, the products were safe.

Inquiry space, 9th September 2020.

Celotex are a major insulation manufacturer. They're a huge corporation. We do not expect to be misled by them [...] We trusted what they told us.

QC. Even though they had a vested interest in making sure you bought the product because they were making it and selling it?

RAY BAILEY. Yeah. Why – how – why would they lie to us?

Inquiry space, 16th November 2020.

CAST MEMBER. Jonathon Roper, Celotex Product Manager and Area Sales Manager.

QC. [You worked for Celotex as a product manager and then an area sales manager.]

Do you accept – I think you do – that you didn't tell your sales team [...] that there had been an earlier fire test of your product that had failed; or that the second test had only passed by reason of the presence of a non-combustible six-millimetre magnesium board [...] in two places [on the test rig] which would serve to stop fire spread [but only on the test rig] [...] That's right, isn't it?

JONATHAN ROPER. That's right, yes [...]

QC. Let's look at the slides [...] If we look at Slide Nine [...] there is no mention of the magnesium [board on the test rig] [...] You knew at the time, surely, that this slide was downright misleading?

JONATHAN ROPER. Yes, I did [...]

QC. Did you realise at the time that if this was how the test was to be described to the market, it would be a fraud on the market?

JONATHAN ROPER. Yes, yeah, I did.

QC. Did you not feel at the time a sense that that was wrong?

JONATHAN ROPER. I felt incredibly uncomfortable with it. I recall going home that evening, and I still lived with my parents at the time and mentioned that to them, and I felt incredibly uncomfortable with what I was being asked to do. Yeah.

QC. Was there nobody [at] Celotex you could have gone to and shared those concerns with?

JONATHAN ROPER. All of the senior management were in that meeting.

Inquiry space, 17th November 2020.

CAST MEMBER. Paul Evans, Celotex Manager of Jonathon Roper.

QC. Are you telling us you had no idea […] about the addition of the six-millimetre magnesium board on the rig […]?

PAUL EVANS. The only thing I knew was that – that I recall is that we changed the thickness of the cladding panel.

QC. Are you sure about that?

PAUL EVANS. Yes.

QC. Be careful here. This isn't just that you can't recall; you're saying, are you, that both Mr Roper in his evidence yesterday and what another of your employee's, Mr Hayes, says are false?

PAUL EVANS. What I'm saying is that I didn't know that we had put a six-mil magnesium [board] […] I didn't know what we were doing here – I didn't know that we were doing it.

On screen:

'The insulation used on Grenfell was made by two companies, Celotext and Kingspan. The Kingspan insulation, which was called Kooltherm K15, had been on the market for some time but they had recently changed its chemical composition. This new-formula K15 was what was used on Grenfell.'

Inquiry space, 23rd November 2020.

CAST MEMBER. Ivor Meredith, former Kingspan Technical Project Manager.

QC. Let's go to your report of the testing of the new version of K15 [...] Under the heading 'Result', we can see you say this: 'By seventeen minutes the top fire barrier had breached and the raging inferno moved up to the top [...] thus failing the simple criteria [of the test] [...] and [then later you write] 'the inspectors had to extinguish the test because it was endangering setting fire to the laboratory' [...] Now, would you agree that it became clear to you very quickly that this new K15 could not repeat the fire performance of old technology K15? [...]

IVOR MEREDITH. I was – I mean, I was shocked, as you can see by my words, that the phenolic was burning ferociously [...]

Inquiry space, 24th November 2020.

QC. Kingspan knew, didn't it, all along that K15 was not a material of limited combustibility; on the contrary, it was a combustible insulation, wasn't it?

IVOR MEREDITH; Yeah. Definitely.

Inquiry space, 30th November 2020.

CAST MEMBER. Philip Heath, Kingspan Division Business Development Director.

QC. Can you help us as to why you didn't say, 'Stop all sales of this product, particularly sales over eighteen metres, we need to do some further investigation'? Why did you not do that?

PHILIP HEATH. I can't recollect why I wouldn't have said that. I don't know why I wouldn't have said that [...]

QC. This is about life safety. Did that not ever occur to you?

PHILIP HEATH. [...] We probably wondered was it just that system that it was failing on at that time, [...] there was a number of things that we were considering at the time as a collective, really [...]

QC. Were there ever any discussions [...] about withdrawing K15, particularly from the above-eighteen-metre market, given its markedly different performance in fire?

PHILIP HEATH. Not that I can recall, no.

QC. Can you help us as to why not? [...]

PHILIP HEATH. I don't know [...]

QC. Is the truth that in fact all you were focused on at that time was desperately trying to obtain some other evidence that K15 could be considered appropriate, so that you could maintain the sales you were already achieving in that market?

PHILIP HEATH. I don't believe we were desperate to be in that market, but we certainly wanted to be in that market [...]

QC. I'm going to ask the question again: in truth, weren't you focused at that time on sales and not focused at all on health and safety?

PHILIP HEATH. I certainly wasn't focused on sales. My role was managing the technical department, the advisory service and the large-scale tests. My role wasn't sales-orientated.

NICK. So, we, we, we heard a noise outside our, our front door, so I started banging on the door. Someone shouted:

'We know you're there.'

Then boom the door goes through. I said I've got my dog here and the guy just said, sorry, let's go. I, I didn't see the fire officers at all I just saw one arm come and grab my wife out of the smoke, another arm come and grab me and then we were just out into the darkness.

I got detached from my wife's waist and I started screaming where's my wife, where's my wife?

And then someone said: 'We've got her.'

I just kept going around and around and around and around and then as you got lower the banister just got hotter and hotter and then the I couldn't even touch the banister it was just pure not molten but boiling metal.

I remember my knees giving way thinking this is it now because I cannot take another breath. I had the, the towel wrapped as far back as I could push it down my throat because every breath was just hot black smoke and then you're thinking this is it. I, I can't, I can't do any more.

02:32, Nick leaves the building.

When I came out and um I had to wait for my wife for ages and ages and four or five officers brought her out of the tower one on each limb.

They'd cut off all my wife's clothes except for one little top so all her trousers, and underwear, shoes all gone, and I had a little towel still, so I just threw it over her. They didn't even stop for me they just carried on. My wife's body was really bruised it was all the skin was weeping and everything. All over. So I, I really don't know what happened.

They put my wife on the red triage and um then they put me on the blue and yellow as in the middle so I kind of collapsed down on the floor there.

I was trying to get up to go to my wife I saw her going onto the red one and then I saw, I saw somebody carrying out CPR and I thought that's it my wife's dead and then they brought her over to me, so we embraced and everything crying, and I was just so happy to see her and then I stood up but then I kind of collapsed.

Then the next thing my wife's disappeared so I'm asking where's my wife, where's my wife?

Inquiry space, 10th September 2018.

FF (Firefighter) Lawson of Willesden Red Watch.

QC. Looking at the instruction you were given, was the level of detail sufficient for your purposes?

FF LAWSON. It got us to where we needed to go. It didn't prepare us for what we found on the eighteenth floor.

[…] We had complete sensory deprivation from the moment of putting our masks on. You could hear muffled voices. We had no visibility. We got up the stairs by feeling up the banisters. It could've been five minutes, could've been ten minutes, I really don't know [...]

QC. [...] As you went up, what was your experience of radio?

FF LAWSON. [...] From probably the moment I put our mask on to the moment we left the building again, it was untenable, couldn't use it. [It just didn't work.]

QC. [...] Given the conditions you encountered on the way up, did this suggest to you that people needed to be evacuated immediately once you got to them on the eighteenth floor?

FF LAWSON. No, I don't make a predisposed decision on the way up there; I take things as I find them when I find them [...] We constantly change decisions based on what we find around us at that given time [...] The first flat we got into was a young lady with three children.

RABIA. Two, two um, two firemen came knocking on the door, er they came in cos I didn't have smoke inside my flat at that time but outside the lobby my front door was, there was no light, it was thick black smoke at this point. So, they came in, shut the door straight away behind them.

FF LAWSON. I would describe her as Middle Eastern wearing a headscarf and you could tell English was not her first language.[23]

RABIA. I was wearing something like this – (*She indicates her hijab.*) just a plain black one. Had my pyjamas underneath and just my scarf on my head. They presumed that I didn't speak English just because I was obviously, I was wearing a scarf. English is my first language. I was born here.

FF LAWSON. I went into her lounge and sat on her sofa [...] I introduced myself. The atmosphere was so clear, I removed my helmet and my smoke hood and my B[reathing] A[pparatus, my BA] mask so I could speak clearly. I also thought it would help calm the children rather than see me in full BA gear. Discussed what was going on outside and that for the moment, the time being, they were safe in this flat.

QC. [...] What consideration did you give to, for example, prioritising the evacuation of the children?

FF LAWSON. In my mind there, the situation where we turned up, to take them outside that flat, I am pretty certain they would've died in my arms on the staircase.

QC. What advice did you give to the lady?

FF LAWSON. I told her to remain calm for her children. I told her to make sure – I told her we had to search the rest of the floor. I told her that her room was obviously clear enough and unaffected enough for me to remove my BA mask, and that she'd be safe until we managed to get someone back to save her.

RABIA. I told them I was pregnant as well. They said to me um okay we are going to knock on your neighbours' doors and we are gonna get you lot all out together. I said okay so I let them go. They said shut the door behind us and put um something on the door to block the smoke from coming.

QC. As you left, what did you say to her?

FF LAWSON. I've no idea.

QC. Did you say you would be back, for example?

FF LAWSON. I told her someone would come back for her, yes.

RABIA. They said they are going to come back for us, and they said so and I let them go.

QC. Did you say you would come back or someone?

FF LAWSON. I said someone would come back for her.

BELLAL. She told me that the firefighters basically told her that they needed more help for a rescue and were going to check on the neighbours but that they were coming back. It was a glimmer of hope and she felt briefly reassured.

FF LAWSON. I remember, once we'd been around the rest of the floor and made our way back to outside her front door deliberating for a good few seconds as to the best course of action, and I still didn't believe I was in a position to save everyone on that floor with just two firefighters [...]

When you're faced with nine people and there's only two of you, me personally, I would find it difficult to ask a parent to

pick two children for me to save. I think that's a decision no
one could happily make. We tried to see – we waited a few
seconds to see if there was an opportunity to get them out in
clearer smoke. Didn't happen. We prioritised radio messages
and I stood on the staircase and yelled for help.

QC. […] What did you expect would happen to the occupants
of flat one-five-two once you'd gone?

FF LAWSON. In all my time in the fire service, I expect flats
and buildings to behave in a certain way.

If I can stand in a room and remove my BA mask and
converse with somebody, I expect that to be the conditions in
the building. I didn't foresee them changing that badly.

QC. Did you assume you would have sufficient time to
complete the search of the floor, get down, report to the
bridgehead, and for fresh crews to be deployed to rescue?

FF LAWSON. Yes, or I wouldn't have done it.

RABIA. So, I then assumed that the firemen is on the other side
of the building and on our floor on side and he is going to
come back. The kids were freaking out.

BELLAL. I was watching the fire spread live on television.

RABIA. It was hard to sort of calm them down. Cos obviously
I didn't know what was going on myself so how can I reassure.

We was all in the sitting room – my sitting room is open-
plan. Then the sparks started coming flying from up and it
dropped on the window ledge and then it just literally after
that it just went full. The fire just, it set fire quickly and then
it just sort of came into the room, came into the kitchen.

BELLAL. The kids were screaming and so Rabia passed them
the phone for me to calm them down – which I tried to do.

I recall Rabia going to the door, she started to have a coughing
attack and she started crying. I think she said something like:

RABIA. No, no, it's pitch black.

BELLAL. I could see the fire spreading across to our flat.
I knew she had to get out. When she described the smoke,

I felt an overwhelming sense of dread. She said she couldn't see her hand in front of her face.

RABIA. The kids were literally pushing the door shut, trying to shut the door back again and I am like literally having to force all three kids er out the door so for them to escape because I was forcing them to go into something dangerous. In their heads they didn't know, they thought they were safe in the house but then the fire was behind them.

BELLAL. Then my phone ran out of battery. I didn't know what had happened to her or the kids. I was in shock, in panic. I started to bang my head out of sheer desperation. My friend grabbed me and calmed me down a bit.

RABIA. We went to the neighbours' house and then they let us in, er I told them what the firemen said she said he had they said the same thing.

BELLAL. I got my battery up again and Rabia called me. She was kind of narrating what was happening. She was saying things like 'our flat is gone' and 'the corridor is full of smoke'. She explained she was in flat one-five-three with our neighbours. She had calmed down a little. She told me, 'Listen, I just need five minutes to pray. I need to ask Allah what to do.'

RABIA. [The neighbours] were just, they were in a bad way, there was two children and three adults, one was another neighbour. They was screaming and shouting and crying one of them, one of them was leaning on the window ledge crying he doesn't want to be burnt alive he wants to be buried.

And I was sitting with my kids in seeing it they are watching that.

The firemen didn't come back, they didn't come back.

Inquiry space, 25th September 2018.

AC (ASSISTANT COMMISIONER) ANDY ROE. [...] I think I arrived a couple of minutes before two-thirty-nine [...] As I was walking towards the command unit, I encountered more and more groups of people who were clearly distressed, clearly horrified [...] Not anger, but agitation, concern that perhaps things weren't being done. You could hear it in the voice. People were asking me, 'What's happening? Are they going inside the building? Are they rescuing?'

[...] It was very obvious that at that point of the incident, there had been an absolute building system failure. I've never seen anything like it [...] The building was gone [...] The facade was entirely alight, every window I could see, there had been a breach of compartmentation. There was no viable way of saving that building.[24]

Inquiry space, 26th September 2018.

[...] I remember thinking very clearly that I wanted to end 'stay put'.

Continuation of the call that started at 02:34:42:

RABIA. Please, tell them to find out what's happening with – they're not going to come. Please, yeah, send them, please.

CRO. All right, then. I'm going to go and tell them. If the situation –

RABIA. Thank you.

CRO. Listen, if the situation gets worse, then give me a ring straight back, okay?

RABIA. It's getting – it's worse now –

CRO (*overspeaking*). I know it – I know it's worse. I know it's worse. But I'm going to tell them – as soon as I put –

RABIA (*overspeaking*). Okay.

CRO (*overspeaking*). – the phone down to you, I'm going to tell the command unit –

RABIA (*overspeaking*). All right. Okay –

CRO (*overspeaking*). – down there to come –

RABIA (*overspeaking*). Okay.

CRO (*overspeaking*). – and – directly up to you, all right?

RABIA (*overspeaking*). Okay. Please –

CRO (*overspeaking*). Okay. Thank you.

RABIA (*overspeaking*). – send them up now.

CRO (*overspeaking*). All right. Okay. Bye-bye.

RABIA. It was like when you dialled and called the operator, she was like she was just trying to brush us off.

She was being very dismissive in the sense that she just wanted us to get off the phone because there is a lot of other nine-nine-nine calls coming in.

AC ANDY ROE. I […] turned to the command unit staff to […] make contact with control, and oddly found I didn't have to because control were on the phone […] A command unit officer […] said:

COMMAND UNIT OFFICER. Control are on the phone asking to end 'stay put' advice, what do you want to do?

AC ANDY ROE. I said: I want to end it anyway, so you can tell them yes and I think we should be advising people they need to make best efforts to escape.

RABIA. I was panicking because I know the fire was next door and it was going so fast – very fast. Naila rang nine-nine-nine and handed me the phone.

On screen:

'"Stay put" was ended at 2:47 when a major incident was finally declared.'

02:48:22.

RABIA. Hello?

CRO. Hello, yeah, your daughter told me that the fire is in the flat next door, is that right?

RABIA. Yeah.

CRO. Listen, you –

RABIA. I called in and someone said they're (*Several inaudible words.*) let them know that (*Inaudible.*) there's four –

CRO (*overspeaking*). Okay. Well listen we're – if the fire's in the flat next door you're going to have to leave, okay, you're going to have to make your way –

RABIA (*overspeaking*). Where? We're on the eighteenth floor –

CRO. Okay.

RABIA. – (*Inaudible.*) thick black smoke.

CRO. I know. Listen, we're not going to be able to get up there to you. You need to leave the flat and get out.

RABIA. I made the decision to leave.

BELLAL. The last call I got from Rabia was when she told me she was going to leave the tower. I could tell she was more certain about leaving than anything else in her life. She told me that she was not waiting there any more and she was going down. I could hear the panic, but she was very firm. She had made up her mind.

RABIA. And then my neighbour she, the mum, she said okay we'll go together so she tried to get towels to wet for her boys. I went to help her to wet it. There was no water pressure, it was, it was literally dripping, and we had to wait ages just to wet the towels.

We wet them and pushed open the door. I picked up my little one, picked her up on my chest. She was three at the time and I just remember holding on to my kids both hands, and she was called monkey because she, she is always like a little monkey, she clings on. So she clung on to me. We couldn't, you couldn't see nothing. It was pitch black.

BELLAL. She was in the middle of saying something when I lost her signal and the call cut off. It was the worst moment of my life. Time stopped.

RABIA. It was thick smoke, pitch black, I couldn't cover my face. I was scared I was going to lose one of the kids just letting go so my towel fell off but I didn't bother picking it up. I just clung on to the kids.

We went down the stairs bit by bit. I was familiar with the stairs because obviously I had lived there for more or less all my life.

Couldn't see anyone. I didn't, I don't even remember seeing my neighbours. It was literally like I was on my own, me. My eldest was very vocal. She kept shouting:

'What floor are we on, what floor are we on?'

And I can remember saying to her: 'Keep calm just keep going.'

BELLAL. I made a prayer when it seemed so bleak. I prayed for each of them. I prayed that I would be thankful if even only one of them survived.

RABIA. My son collapsed. He just was, the smoke got to him and he just fell unconscious. And I was standing there, it was, well for me it felt like a lifetime.

A fireman came out from that floor that we was standing. I saw them cos he had a helmet with a light. He picked my son up and he went running down the stairs with him and I just carried on going with the girls. And the fireman just kept saying to me:

'Keep going.

Just keep going.'

BELLAL. I began to call my family and friends to make sure they were watching the different exits in case they appeared. The time that passed felt like an eternity.

RABIA. At the time we was obviously, I was walking slow because I was pregnant and holding three kids. So, I wasn't running. I wasn't running.

We got to the first floor then we saw light and I just thought, okay, we are okay, and with that we are out.

They took my little girl off me, the fireman took her off me, and then we are literally had to be escorted one by one out of the building.

Riot shields had to be above our heads because the things
were just dropping, I mean it was just the amount of debris
just kept dropping, I didn't even see my son.

03:18, Rabia leaves the building.

I remember looking up at the building as soon as I got out
and it was literally alight. I couldn't see any bit of it that
wasn't on fire. Then we walked through, and I saw my son
on the floor. I was running for him. But they was giving him
oxygen and stuff. They, they just picked him up and put him
in an ambulance and they wouldn't let me go with him,
I didn't know if he was alive.

BELLAL. My friend called me. He was shouting down the
phone. 'I've got Ayesha in my hands. I'm holding her. She's
here, say hello to Daddy, say hello to Daddy.'

RABIA. I was just getting in the ambulance and I remember my
daughter taking off her oxygen and just giving it to me. At
the hospital I remember them saying we want they wanted to
take the children to another room I said no, no they are with
me and after I don't know what happened. Apparently,
I collapsed.

ANTONIO. I was pacing continuously. Assessing, checking,
obviously the adrenalin keeps you going.

You could see that the puffs of smoke coming in from these
beautiful nice windows coming in filling up the room with
smoke.

I've got pictures. Evidence of, evidence that, you know,
somebody's trying to kill me here, meaning the company that
did the refurbishment. You know what I mean.

NATASHA. I walked back down the passage into the bathroom
and put the plug in the bath and run the tap. And I remember
my partner saying to me: 'What the hell are you doing?' And
obviously you won't use this word, but my exact words
were: 'The house is gonna be fucked, what's a bit of water?'
That was my exact words.

And, just proceeded to let the bath overflow.

ANTONIO. When I realised that the water was coming down at four, four-thirty in the morning, I switched off all the, the, the television, electrical appliances, everything off. Fridge, cooker, fire, you know, water, you know, switch off, switch off everything...

NATASHA. I remember thinking: 'Shit, I've flooded Antonio again.'

ANTONIO. ....except for one, ah, socket with my phone charging. Because I want to keep the line open with Christopher.

NATASHA. At one point I was laying on the floor trying to keep my, you know, keep daughter calm. I get a phone call from my sister to say, she's with a fireman and they're coming up to get me. And this is now about half past four. She told me they were outside my door.

And then literally opened the door and we were obviously out lightning quick. Um, but it was pitch black. I couldn't tell you how many firemen. Couldn't see a thing. So, my partner obviously was in front.

FIREFIGHTER. Walk towards the torch.

NATASHA. I've seen him go. He's holding my daughter and we've gone literally out, down.

But it was just the sheer fear of not knowing what was going on downstairs. And we've come down, come down again, and then at that point we've all stumbled. My partner stumbled, my daughter, the fireman's taken my daughter off him because there was a body on the stairs. Then I've come down, I've done the same thing. A fireman's held me up. Then we keep going down and then all of a sudden, the lights come back on, on the stairs.

04:47:21, Natasha leaves the building.

I distinctly remember seeing a lady sort of, I believe she was a firewoman, or she could have been a man, but she, I remember her looking up as we come down and then as we got down, there was just a row of firefighters. And I remember looking at some of the faces and I mean they are complete blank faces,

I couldn't, I wouldn't recognise one of them if you put them in a line-up. But I remember looking at the look of, you don't know how lucky you are, you're one of the lucky ones.

I was third-from-last out. Antonio was second-from-last, I think.

ANTONIO. I called the hotel, telling them what is happening, that I will not go to work. I said, listen, I'm not coming because this, this and this.

Around five o'clock, for the first time I saw the, the, the flames, then the room, ah, filling up with smoke very quickly.

I was a little bit, you know, because, you know, you it's a lot of a long time, you know, and then I said to Christopher, Christopher, get me somebody now and he said, okay, okay. They, they, they pushed him back and, basically, he, he, he told the police, fuck off, and he managed to run next to the tower to two firemen and then, ah, I spoke to him and said, okay, I know, we know, still on the tenth floor, right, yes, yes, okay, okay. Somebody's going to get you quite, quite, very soon, okay.

Someody knocked hard at the door. I let him in straight away and they came in heavily equipped, big men with the, ah, oxygen. Two of them. Oxygen masks and with a, the helmet and so, and they said: 'How many of you, mate?'

There's only one, me.

They said 'Okay, we're gonna do the following. Um, I'm gonna be in the front. You grab me in the back. My colleague will hold you in the back as well you're gonna be in between us and we will go downstairs together, okay?'

And I said, okay, let me reiterate what you said, because I wanted to make sure I understood properly. You want me to hold you like this and, and, and like that?

They said 'Yes, yes, like this. So, then, ah, okay, ready, ready, let's go.'

I had my rucksack, I had my jacket up to here, which I still have here, the shoes properly tied and, ah, before that the last call from my son, Christopher said, Pappi, Pappi, there is a pair of, ah, and I've got them here as well, swimming goggles in my room, and his room was full of smoke. I went in and I knew where the drawer is and I, I, I went through, and I found them. So, basically, I wear the ah, these little goggles.

So, ah, I hold the fireman.The heat was absolutely intense, the wine had popped open. It was like a, like Hell... I could see nothing, totally following him.

At one stage I tripped over something and I couldn't go any further. So, the guy behind me, he freed me and, um, and in two minutes we went down. A lot of mud, a lot of water, a lot of rubbish, a lot of debris and water coming down like a – (*Blows air.*) heavy rain coming down on, on, ah, on, on, on my head.

06:05, Antonio leaves the building.

We got out. Well, I said, thank you, thank you to everybody and then I turned around, they had gone back upstairs again. Unbelievable.

HANAN. Later, when it was light, I went to the rugby club. A woman I didn't know came out and suggested we make a list of who was in the tower and hadn't yet been found. I gave her Abdulaziz's name, and she wrote it down.

There must have been a mix-up because Abdulaziz's name somehow got onto the community safe list of people who had been found, so there were rumours circulating that they were safe. We didn't get final confirmation until weeks later that Abdulaziz, Faouzia, Yasin, Nur Huda and Mehdi had all died in the fire.

BELLAL. I went to King's College Hospital to see Aymen and Naila.

They were in opposite beds, unmoving, they had tubes in their mouths and these blue padded boots, they were both in deep comas. I felt a guilt that I had not been there for them. An iman was sent to pray over Aymen, that's how touch-and-go it was.

ED. There's film of me at like eight o'clock in the morning, ITV has got this, of me shouting, we told them this was going to happen and where is the help? No one has come to help us.

Didn't sleep for like three days. I might have got into bed, but I didn't sleep.

NATASHA. I remember going to sleep about three o'clock the next night and remember waking up at six o'clock and going and sitting in my mum's garden and having a cigarette. And I remember a robin coming. And my nan had passed away the year before. Um, since my nan had passed, this robin comes and visits my mum regularly, so my mum's got it in her head it's my nan and which is you know fine. I really believe my nan was with me that night anyway.

Not only did I lose my home, not only did I lose neighbours and friends, that night I lost my uncle, Steve Power, my mum's brother. He lived four floors above me and he never made it out.

RABIA. I woke up three weeks later. By then all my three children were out of hospital.

NICK. Our other neighbours, Amal and her daughter, and um Marjorie and Ernie um they, they all perished. Debbie from the sixteenth as well. You know Debbie used to come to our house sit with my wife chitter, chitter, chitter chat.

TURUFAT. I had my sentimental things that I will never never replace and you know it might sound small but it's not it's not small. You know something I treasure from my dad who is no longer with us. And I had a stillbirth when I was six months and they will take a picture after and the the thumbprint, the foot, everything, yeah, a full album. They give you to check it whenever you ready. You always pick up you wanna take but it's not ready yet so you put it back so yeah...

MAHER. When my wife came to UK she brought a picture from before I had polio: the only one before polio when I was five. And it's gone with the fire. I'm really very sad about this until today.

And now I expect a fire to happen wherever I am. That's the truth. Whenever I go anywhere, in absolutely any situation, I watch videos on YouTube that show how a disabled person can escape.

NATASHA. My house was relatively intact. There's quite a lot of smoke damage. All I asked for initially was three birds that, plastic Christmas birds that belonged to my nan. Budgie things. Light blue, red gold that used to just clip on the Christmas tree. They're as old as me which is why I really, really wanted them back. A mirror that was my nan's and my daughter's doll's pram and my other daughter's car keys. They were only things I wanted.

MAHER. Since Grenfell me and my wife don't celebrate our anniversary any more.

NATASHA. I'd give anything to turn the clocks back and ensure that all seventy-one of those people come out of that building.

HANAN. My brother had kept telling me to say it was going to be alright so that his son Mehdi wouldn't panic. I said, 'It'll be fine, it'll be fine.' I now feel guilty about this, that I kept saying it was going to be okay even though I knew it wasn't.

TIAGO. It sounds weird but Captain America inspired me to become a better activist after the fire. It didn't matter who was going up against you as long as you stayed true to your morals. At the end of the day the most important thing is human life and human decency.

TURUFAT. We have that one box given from the tower, just one box. It's the size of if you have a delivery small. It has that smell of the night so it's just it hits you really, really hits you – we don't want it just destroyed but we don't know when are we going to open it. Maybe… I don't know when it's the right time. We keep it under the table. We don't have any storage so it has to be sitting there and we get now and then question from our son you know 'Why you not opening?' I know just keep telling him one day, one day.

NICK. Pily's death was the seventy-second from the fire. She never recovered and she passed the following January and it's truly written in the stars because she took her last breath as her son walked in the, in the room. He said what's wrong, I said she's just gone. I said just this second. Yeah. But she'd waited for him. Her funeral was amazing. I just put it out that everybody's invited and don't wear black. They brought her in a horse-, a horse-drawn coach and we got like five limousines, we've got quite a big family and we drove behind the horse and carriage. We came along up Ladbroke Grove and then we pulled up outside the fire station and er they'd brought the fire engines out and there was a guard of honour. They all had white roses and they all came over and laid the white roses. And then we continued up to um Harrow Road and arrived at the crematorium and I just couldn't believe my eyes, there were hundreds of people there, hundreds. Everyone colourful.

We hear music as a section of the audience is moved.

A screen comes down.

The names of the seventy-two who died are projected on the screen.

Here follows the names:[25]

1.
Abdeslam Sebbar
Ali Yawar Jafari
Denis Murphy
Mohammed Al-Haj Ali
Jeremiah Deen
Zainab Deen
Steven Power
Sheila
Joe (Joseph) Daniels
Husna Begum
Kamru Miah
Mohammed Hamid
Mohammed Hanif
Rabeya Begum
Forever in Our Hearts

2.
Khadija Khaloufi
Vincent Chiejina
Fatemeh Afrasehabi

Sakineh Afrasehabi
Isaac Paulos
Hamid Kani
Berkti Haftom
Biruk Haftom
Gary Maunders
Deborah (Debbie) Lamprell
Forever in Our Hearts

3.
Ernie Vital
Marjorie Vital
Maria Del-Pilar Burton
Amal Ahmedin
Amaya Tuccu-Ahmedin
Amna Mahmud Idris
Mohamednur Tuccu
Victoria King
Alexandra Atala
Mary Mendy
Khadija Saye
Forever In Our Hearts

4.
Farah Hamdan Belkadi
Leena Belkadi
Malak Belkadi
Omar Belkadi
Jessica Urbano
Ligaya Moore
Abdulaziz El Wahabi
Faouzia El-Wahabi
Mehdi El-Wahabi
Nur Huda El Wahabi
Yasin El Wahabi
Forever in Our Hearts

5.
Logan Gomes
Firdaws Hashim
Hashim Kedir
Nura Jemal

Yahya Hashim
Yaqub Hashim
Fatima Choucair
Mierna Choucair
Nadia Choucair
Sirria Choucair
Zainab Choucair
Bassem Choucair
Forever in Our Hearts

6.
Anthony (Tony) Disson
Mariem Elgwahry
Eslah Elgwahry
Raymond Bernard aka Moses
Gloria Trevisan
Marco Gottardi
Fethia Hassan
Hania Hassan
Rania Ibrahim
Hesham Rahman
Mohamed (Saber) Amied Neda
Abufras Ibrahim
Isra Ibrahim
Fathia Ali Ahmed Elsanosi
Forever in Our Hearts

A short documentary followed straight on from Act Two, with the following real people speaking, alongside footage of the tower and the Silent Walk.

FERUZA AFEWERKI, *bereaved*
TIAGO ALVES, *Flat 105*
NICK BURTON, *Flat 156*
ED DAFFARN, *Flat 134*
FATIMA EL-GUENUNI, *psychotherapist and mother of Bellal El-Guenuni*
MAHER KHOUDAIR, *Flat 64*
KARIM MUSSILHY, *bereaved*
ANTONIO RONCOLATO, *Flat 72*
HANAN WAHABI, *Flat 66, bereaved*
TURUFAT YILMA, *Flat 44*

NICK. I lived in that tower with my wife for thirty-three years. Then it's gone in a second. Everything that you own, all the memories, you know, those things that are sacred to you. And then the realisation that your neighbours, your friends that you can't find, they, they may be still in there.

KARIM. Seventy-two people died. The world watched. Eighteen kids. Eighteen children passed away.

TURUFAT. They left us the whole twenty-four hours outside. Really. And there was not a sign of RBKC who supposed to look after, you know, us. The community.

ED. We live in the twenty-first century, in the sixth-richest country in the world. And our government and our local authority abandoned us.

FATIMA. It was chaotic. It was unplanned, unconscious. They didn't have a register.

KARIM. I never saw anybody from the TMO or RBKC. I expected to see somebody somewhere in a high-viz with a

clipboard, you know, taking down people's names and
details. And that never happened.

FATIMA. The whole housing response was also very chaotic.
People were put in hotel rooms. You had my son and his wife
and the three children all living in one room for probably
nearly six months.

MAHER (*speaking in Arabic with subtitles*). All of us were in
one room. Me and my wife and the three girls.

KARIM. Initially, when it happened, everybody who wasn't
identified in the hospitals was classed as missing. So Uncle
was technically missing up until the end of July. By about
the second or third week, I remember I was walking around
constantly, that's all I did, was just walking around trying to
talk to people and see if I could find out any other bits of
information about him.

I saw this T-shirt that the firefighters had left. It was written
with, with a black marker or something along the lines of to,
to all that was on the twenty-first floor and above was 'Sorry
we couldn't get to you.' And it was at that moment that
I realised that Uncle probably had passed away and he was
still in the tower.

HANAN. Why did it happen to this community and not South
Kensington as opposed to North Kensington, for example?
Which is another thing that I'm passionate about, as to why
it happened in this part of the borough.

FATIMA. That night just highlighted the level of racial or racist
tones within, within systems. I've never heard of any
emergency response that had riot police accompany the
ambulance and, you know, and the firefighters.

KARIM. The police's priority at the time, especially during the
early days, were to try to control this perception that they
had that we were going to riot, that all of us were going to,
you know, tear down the city.

The council were well aware of my uncle's conditions. They
knew he was, he had mobility issues. They knew what his
disabilities were, but they still stuck him on the twenty-third

floor. Even the fight to try to get some new laws and legislations put in for disabled people and have sort of evacuation plans for them has been a fight. It's not something that the government agreed to.

NICK. You can put man on the moon, but it's an impossibility to have a list of people in the tower that cannot escape.

KARIM. I'm not an activist. I never was an activist. And I don't want to be an activist. I'm just somebody whose uncle was murdered, and I'm not having it.

ANTONIO. You know, we find out afterwards that the council didn't want the government to be involved because they wanted to show that they could manage it and they could not. They were totally unprepared.

ED. Central government had a series of 999 calls over the past three decades that they chose to ignore. And had they acted, had they tightened up the regulations, we wouldn't be sitting here having this conversation today.

MAHER. It was negligence, total negligence. And indifference towards peoples' lives.

HANAN. I believe that it's a generational impact. So what's impacted me will impact my children, will impact my children's children, even those who are not even born yet.

KARIM. The government has allowed these corporations, these companies, to behave the way that they do.

TURUFAT. Through the Inquiry, the evidence is there. So it's all about money and greed.

ED. I have no ability to reconcile with the perpetrators, with the likes of Arconic, Kingspan and Celotex who since the fire have not shown remorse, have not shown contrition.

KARIM. Arconic knew the dangers of their material, but they targeted the UK market specifically because they knew the regulations in place were so blasé.

FERUZA. When the unimaginable happens, we have to look at the system and think 'This is not working.'

TIAGO. It was the people from the local community who were trying to make sure that we were fed, that we were hydrated, and that we had clothes on our back.

TURUFAT. That will stay with me forever.

FERUZA. I think something that I discovered just how beautiful our community is. We are more than our trauma. You can go through intense devastation and still be a whole person.

KARIM. It felt like the whole country came, came to aid.

FERUZA. And for me it has been the response of the people, of the community of Grenfell, and the surrounding community in London, how people have come together and how people have shown just so much compassion and care for the survivors, the bereaved and the local community. That as much as it felt like our lives ended on that day, that we're still here and that we're still living memorials of those that we've lost.

There is a quote that I really love by Dr Cornel West, and it says, 'Justice is what love looks like in public.'

TURUFAT. But for us, for us, for me as well, justice is when all these buildings which are covered by the same cladding, when they remove and they change the legalisation and everything, then that is a justice.

HANAN. There is still cladding on buildings till today which another aspect of justice. It needs to come off and it needs to be paid for.

TIAGO. Changes need to be made within local government, within central government, and within all the other institutions around building regulations. So that's one form of justice. There is also criminal justice.

NICK. There's no justice for the dead. Justice is different for everybody.

FATIMA. For me, justice also means change, change within systems, valuing people, valuing people as human beings. First and foremost, we all deserve to feel safe in our homes.

ANTONIO. Yes, I want and I really hope that we will have justice, that the people have not died in vain. But I will not believe it until I see it.

HANAN. A tragedy that happened in this country needs to be included in the national curriculum. People need to remember it. People need to know what happened, the same way we remember the Great Fire of London, we need to remember Grenfell Tower Fire.

ANTONIO. Justice for me would mean bringing all those people responsible at any level to account, and their freedom be taken away.

FERUZA. My focus is how do we heal and how do we rebuild our lives and become the people that we always meant to be? I think it did surprise me, the strength and the resilience from the response of the community, and I saw how it kind of put courage in me when I went on my first silent walk and I was able to come back to the tower, it was because I knew that there was a community gathering every month walking in silence, and I wanted to experience that, that connection. Just to know that you're not alone, that they can show up the way they did, where people did expect them to riot and, and, rightfully so, because murder had taken place, and the fact that they were walking with such dignity and compassion and care. So the silence of the walk was really important to me because when that kind of violence happens around you, you need gentleness. You need a human approach. When you're grieving, you just need to feel safe. So I found that was a lot of power in the silence.

TURUFAT. Everybody can be a voice for the voiceless. You don't have to go and talk, but you can, you know, be part of that group and then you can be the member, you can involve. You can contribute whatever you can contribute. Yes.

NICK. This is 'Zoom out and have a look what's happening' on a global scale, on a big scale of who these, these monsters are.

ED. So for me, the most important thing that an audience could take away from seeing the play and engaging with, with what happened to Grenfell Tower on the 14th June 2017 is to essentially keep us in their hearts, not to forget the very human stories, but also to make sure that Grenfell and the crimes that were committed against our community are not forgotten.

MAHER. I want everyone to pay attention If someone comes to do work on your house or building ask them 'What is that? Has it been inspected? I need to see proof that this material isn't hazardous for my family or for the building.'

ANTONIO. Don't just allow things to be put upon you, but be part of the decision-making of, at any level. Don't forget that many politicians ultimately want our vote, do come and knock our door when it is convenient for them. And they promised us so many things and we have to make sure that we hold to, hold them to account if they do not deliver.

FATIMA. Compassion and belonging and connection to your neighbourhoods, your communities is key.

KARIM. So have a look at your share portfolios as well. Some people don't even realise that they have pensions in Kingspan or Arconic or Celotex. The system isn't broken. The system was built specifically this way to keep us where we are and them where they are. And we need you to see yourselves in us, meaning that we are trying to move on with our lives.

We don't live in these in these awful buildings any more, but you do, your families do, your friends do. The fight needs to be continued by you. But if we just sit down, watch these plays and watch these documentaries and say, 'Oh, what a tragedy, that was sad', and then forget about it a day later, then this is never going to change.

HANAN. Press that domino. The domino effect. I want to see change. I would like to see justice. And I would like you to help us, to help us to remember, to never forget what happened, and to create that change.

Endnotes

1. youtu.be/hS1H-Pd_aog

2. youtu.be/aM8lzqsRn64 from 06:12 minutes to 06:37 minutes

3. grenfellactiongroup.wordpress.com/2012/08/14/a-special-invitation/

4. grenfellactiongroup.wordpress.com/2013/02/21/another-fire-safety-scandal/

5. Text taken from ITN news report

6. QC is Counsel to the Inquiry throughout

7. grenfellactiongroup.wordpress.com/2015/04/12/grenfell-community-unite-request-public-meeting-with-tmorydon/

8. Taken from her Inquiry evidence, 8 November 2018

9. Taken from his Inquiry evidence, 21 April 2021

10. Taken from her witness statement

11. This call and all subsequent control-room officer conversations contains public-sector information licensed under the Open Government License v.3

12. From his witness statement unless otherwise stated

13. Taken from her witness statement

14. Taken from her witness statement

15. Taken from Sir Martin Moore-Bick's report – her testimony or witness statement

16. QC reads this whole call in the Inquiry

17. Here and in other places where it says 'overspeaking', both people are talking simultaneously so what they say overlaps

18. Taken from the report by Sir Martin Moore-Bick of the first phase of the Grenfell Tower Inquiry

19. Schmidt talked French throughout. QC's words were interpreted for him and his replies interpreted back

20. This sentence is taken from his witness statement

21. Joseph Daniels died in his smoke-logged flat

22. This is, in fact, Moore-Bick asking the questions here

23. Taken from Firefighter Gregory Lawson's witness statement

24. Taken from his Inquiry evidence, 25th September 2018

25. The names are in the order in which the Silent Walk reads them. The numbers indicate a new reader for each group. At the Silent Walk they also say 'Forever in Our Hearts' at the end of each group

Grenfell United

Grenfell United is a group of survivors and bereaved families of the Grenfell Tower fire. Founded in the days after the fire, the families work to rebuild their community and campaign for truth, justice and change. Grenfell United has an elected committee that seeks to represent survivors and bereaved families.

On the night of the 14 June 2017, our lives changed forever. Seventy-two innocent men, women and children died at the hands of corruption and greed.

To this day, we are still fighting for justice. We are still fighting for change. It's a battle because we are fighting against a government, a system, institutions and companies that do not care.

We are fighting for criminal charges and justice for our seventy-two loved ones who lost their lives. Grenfell was no accident, every single death could and should have been avoided. Those responsible must be brought to justice.

We are fighting...

- For the government and all responsible parties to implement the Inquiry recommendations from both the Phase 1 and Phase 2 reports, to ensure another Grenfell never happens again.

- For social-housing culture to change; for residents to be treated with respect, their complaints heard, for everyone to be safe in their homes.

- For Personal Emergency Evacuation Plans for disabled residents, to ensure they are able to leave their homes safely in an emergency.

- For INQUEST's National Oversight Mechanism, to mandate recommendations from inquiries becoming law.
- For the Hillsborough Law, to fix the broken justice system and ensure bereaved and survivors are properly supported.

Grenfell is not restricted to us. Whilst it took seventy-two of our dear ones away from us, scarred us mentally and physically, and broke our community, it also exposed corruption. It exposed failure; it exposed indifference to us.

Our fight is your fight. We all have a responsibility to hold them to account. We all have a need to come together and protect each other from this happening to anyone else.

Stand united with us. Follow us on Twitter, Instagram, sign up to our newsletter and keep in touch with our campaign. Together we are stronger.

Our seventy-two remain forever in our hearts.

grenfellunited.org.uk

Self-care

'Caring for myself is not self-indulgence, it is self-preservation, and that is an act of political warfare.' *Audre Lorde, a Black feminist and pioneer of self-care*

'The concept of self-care comes from the Black feminist movement. Self-care is important because it's about recognising that we experience discrimination and oppression because of how others react to who we are, or what we've experienced. Self-care is a choice to listen to our needs and look after ourselves, so we are able to keep going and live our best lives, despite the difficulties we experience in life and how they make us feel.' *Clean Break*

Self-care guides

www.samaritans.org/how-we-can-help/contact-samaritan/self-help

www.sarsas.org.uk/support-and-information/sarsas-self-help-guides

www.thesurvivorstrust.org/understanding-healing

My Little Book of Coping Skills

https://shout.ams3.cdn.digitaloceanspaces.com/giveusashout/media/documents/coping_skills_final2022.pdf

Anna Freud Self-care Guide

www.annafreud.org/on-my-mind/self-care

This resource hub has been created for young people, but it contains lots of self-care tips and suggestions which anyone could find useful.

Managing Flashbacks

www.napac.org.uk/flashbacks

https://www.thesurvivorstrust.org/Handlers/Download.ashx?ID
MF=3cbb806f-2e82-44df-8207-2ee8d8567948

Although aimed at victims and survivors of sexual violence,
these articles suggest ways of dealing with flashbacks, and how
to support yourself when you may be recalling a traumatic
incident that happened to you.

Other mental-health charities and sources of support

www.mind.org.uk

www.samaritans.org

www.giveusashout.org

www.youngminds.org.uk

*This advice is based on the National Theatre's self-care guide
for* Grenfell: in the words of survivors.